TOP 10
BEIJING

ANDREW HUMPHREYS

D0348113

DK
EYEWITNESS TRAVEL

Left **Tian'an Men** Center **Temple of Heaven** Right **Summer Palace**

LONDON, NEW YORK,
MELBOURNE, MUNICH AND DELHI
www.dk.com

Produced by Brazil Street

Reproduced by Colourscan, Singapore
Printed and bound in Italy by Graphicom

First published in Great Britain in 2007
by Dorling Kindersley Limited
80 Strand, London WC2R 0RL
A Penguin Company

A CIP catalogue record is available
from the British Library.

ISBN 978-1-40531-786-3

Within each Top 10 list in this book,
no hierarchy of quality or popularity
is implied. All 10 are, in the editor's
opinion, of roughly equal merit.

Contents

Beijing's Top 10

The information in this DK Eyewitness Top 10 Travel Guide is checked regularly.
Every effort has been made to ensure that this book is as up-to-date as possible at the time
going to press. Some details, however, such as telephone numbers, opening hours, prices
gallery hanging arrangements and travel information are liable to change. The publishers
cannot accept responsibility for any consequences arising from the use of this book, nor fe
any material on third party websites, and cannot guarantee that any website address in th
book will be a suitable source of travel information. We value the views and suggestions o
our readers very highly. Please write to: Publisher, DK Eyewitness Travel Guides,
Dorling Kindersley, 80 Strand, London, Great Britain WC2R 0RL.

Cover: Front – **DK Images:** Chen Chao bl; Colin Sinclair clb; **Getty Images:** The Image Bank/Yann Lay
main. Spine - **DK Images:** Chen Chao b. Back – **DK Images:** Colin Sinclair cra, cla; **Getty Images:** Sto
Jean-Marc Truchet ca.

eft **Foil-baked fish, Han Cang** Center **World of Suzie Wong** Right **Mahjong players, Hou Hai**

Forbidden City Right **Lama Temple**

BEIJING'S TOP 10

BEIJING'S TOP 10

Beijing's Highlights

At the heart of Beijing is tradition, given physical form in the mighty Forbidden City, from where successive imperial dynasties have ruled since the 15th century. Neighboring Tian'an Men Square is the China of recent history, of red-flag socialism and Mao. But this is also a city on the move, as an all-pervading spirit of change makes Beijing the most 21st-century of capitals.

Forbidden City
So called because at one time only members of the imperial court were allowed inside, this is one of the largest and greatest palace complexes ever built *(see pp8–11).*

Temple of Heaven
Originally the venue for annual winter solstice sacrifices, which were performed by successive emperors to ensure ample harvests, the temple remains Beijing's most recognizable icon *(see pp12–13).*

Tian'an Men Square
The world's largest public square is not pretty, but it is surrounded by august cultural and political institutions, and it is also the final resting place of Chairman Mao Zedong *(see pp14–15).*

Lama Temple
The largest and most spectacular of the city's temples is a working lamasery, home to monks from Mongolia and Tibet *(see pp16–17).*

Bei Hai Park
The most beautiful of Beijing's many city parks is laid out around a central lake, first dug out in the 12th century, with the excavated earth used to create a central island. The famed Kublai Khan ruled his empire from a palace here *(see pp18–19).*

Previous pages **Red flags flying on Tian'an Men Square**

Hou Hai
By day visitors take rickshaw tours around the back lanes for a glimpse of fast-disappearing old Beijing; by night, attention shifts to the area's lakeside bars and restaurants *(see pp20–21)*.

Summer Palace
Beijing summers are unbearably hot, so the imperial court would exchange the Forbidden City for this semi-rural retreat with its ornate pavilions, gardens, and temples, ranged around the cool expanse of Kunming Lake *(see pp22–3)*.

798 Art District
When former electronic components factory 798 became a venue for cutting-edge contemporary art it kick-started a neighborhood trend for converting industrial spaces into galleries and chic cafés and bars *(see pp24–5)*.

Ming Tombs
Thirty miles (45 km) northwest of Beijing is the vast burial site of 13 of China's 16 Ming emperors. One of the underground tombs can be visited but most impressive of all is the Sacred Way, with its 12 pairs of stone guardians *(see pp26–7)*.

Great Wall
"Great" is something of an understatement; the wall is nothing less than spectacular. Clamber up the perilously sloping carriageways to one of the crowning watchtowers and the experience is also quite literally breath-taking *(see pp28–9)*.

TOP10 Forbidden City

Officially known as the Palace Museum, this magnificent complex is a grand monument to the 24 emperors who ruled from its halls over a period of almost 500 years. The symbolic center of the Chinese universe, the palace was the exclusive domain of the imperial court from its completion in 1420 until the last of the emperors was forced to abdicate at the beginning of the 20th century. The modern world intruded in 1949, when the public were finally admitted through the palace gates.

Bronze guardian lion

Glazed panel with lotus and mandarin ducks

☕ The Forbidden City has its own branch of Starbucks.

✿ Most visitors buy their entrance tickets at the Meridian Gate, but to avoid the lengthy queues you could enter the Forbidden City from the north via the Gate of Divine Prowess, and visit in reverse.

North of Tian'an Men Square
* Map L3
* 6513 2255
* Subway: Tian'an Men Xi or Tian'an Men Dong
* Open: Apr 16–Oct 15 8:30am–5pm daily. Oct 16–Apr 15 8:30am–4:30pm daily
* Admission: Apr 1–Oct 31 ¥60. Nov 1–Mar 31 ¥40. There are additional charges for certain halls
* Audio guides are available for ¥40
* www.dpm.org.cn

Top 10 Features

1. Meridian Gate
2. Golden Water
3. Gate of Supreme Harmony
4. Hall of Supreme Harmony
5. Hall of Preserving Harmony
6. Gate of Heavenly Purity
7. Inner Court
8. Imperial Garden
9. Western Palaces
10. Eastern Palaces

1 Meridian Gate
In Chinese it is the Wu Men. This is the traditional entrance to the palaces. From the balcony *(above)* the emperor would review his armies and perform ceremonies marking the start of the new lunar year.

2 Golden Water
Five marble bridges, symbolizing the five cardinal virtues of Confucianism, span the Golden Water, which flows from west to east in a course designed to resemble the jade belt worn by the court officials.

3 Gate of Supreme Harmony
The fourth and final great gate *(below)* gives access into the Outer Court, the heart of the Forbidden Cit The gate is guarded by tw large bronze lions, classic imperial symbols of powe and dignity. The lion on th right *(top)* is the male; the one on the left with a cub under its foot is the fema

Hall of Supreme Harmony

Raised on a triple tier of marble terraces, this largest of halls houses a sandalwood throne *(right)*, used in the coronations of 24 emperors.

Hall of Preserving Harmony

The most spectacular aspect of this hall is the great carved ramp on the north side, sculpted with dragons and clouds, and made from a single piece of marble weighing more than 200 tons.

Gate of Heavenly Purity

The only building *(above)* in the whole palace not to have been burnt down at least once, and thus the oldest hall of all. It is the boundary between the Outer Court (official) and Inner Court (private).

Inner Court

The Inner Court *(left)* is more intimate than the formal Outer Court, because this is where the emperor, empress, and the many concubines actually lived.

Western Palaces

Much of the western bank of the complex is off limits, but some of the halls neighboring the Inner Court are visitable, including the Palace of Eternal Spring, where *trompe-l'oeil* paintings at the ends of passageways make them appear infinitely extended.

Eastern Palaces

East of the Inner Court are smaller halls where the emperor's harem lived. Also here is the well down which the Empress Cixi *(see p23)* had her nephew's favorite concubine thrown.

Imperial Garden

The emperor Qianlong wrote that, "Every ruler, when he has finished his public duties, must have a garden in which he can stroll, and relax his heart." This formal garden, the oldest in the Forbidden City, has two beautiful pavilions *(above)*.

The Last Emperor

Pu Yi, ascended the throne at the age of three in 1908, but his brief reign was brought to an early end in 1912 by a new Republican government. The young ex-emperor continued to live in the Forbidden City until ejected in 1924. He was later imprisoned under the Communists, until Mao granted him amnesty in 1959. He died in 1967, after working for seven years as a gardener.

For more places of interest in the vicinity of the Forbidden City
See pp66–9

Left **Nine-dragon screen** Right **Imperial throne**

Forbidden City Collections

Musical instruments
In true imperial fashion, the more lavish the musical entertainment, the more glory it reflected on the emperor. Court musicians used gongs of all sizes and *guqins* (zithers), wooden flutes, and heavy bronze bells adorned with dragons, as well as the unusual *sheng*, a Sherlock Holmes-style pipe with reeds of different lengths sprouting from the top. The collection is displayed in the Silver Vault of the Imperial Palace, on the west side of the Outer Court.

Scientific instruments
Enlightened Qing emperor Kangxi (1654–1722) appointed Europeans as court officials, and instructed his imperial workshops to copy Western scientific instruments. These included the first calculator, astronomical and drawing tools, sun dials, moon dials, and a special table with measurements and scientific notations scratched on each side leaf, made especially for the imperial studies. The instruments are part of the Imperial Treasures of the Ming and Qing Dynasties exhibit, on the west side of the Inner Court.

Stone drums
The Hall of Moral Cultivation holds the palace's collection of stone drums. These are enormous tom-tom shaped rocks that bear China's earliest stone inscriptions dating back to 374 BC. These ideographic carvings are arranged in four-character poems, which commemorate the glorious pastureland and successful animal husbandry made possible by the Emperor Xiangong's benevolence.

Butterfly brooch

Jewelry
Also in the Hall of Moral Cultivation are three of the six halls of jewelry (head north for rooms four through six), including the only hall to display actual jewelry rather than agate cups or jade sculpture. Hall number three has thick jade rings, lapis lazuli court beads, elaborate headdresses made of gold filigree phoenixes, and surprisingly, jadeite Christian rosary beads.

Beijing Opera
The pleasantly named Pavilion of Cheerful Melodies sports a three-story stage large enough to accommodate one thousand actors. It was once rigged with pulleys and trapdoors to create dramatic entrances for supernatural characters. The exhibits include a behind-the-scenes model stage, as well as costumes, instruments, scripts, and cast lists. There are screens showing reconstructions of old court performances.

Jade
The Hall of Quintessence was once where dowager empresses went to die; it now exhibits jade artifacts spanning thousands of years. Pieces range from simple cups and ladles to enormous and intricate sculptures of Buddhas in traditional scenic settings. The Chinese considered working this "hard" stone a metaphor for character development and the pursuit of perfection.

Daily life of the concubines
Every three years, court officials would select girls between the ages of 13 and 17 to join the eight ranks of imperial concubines. The Yonghe Pavilion exhibits clothing, games, herbal medicine, and a food distribution chart relating to the young imperial consorts, as well as the all-important "wedding night bed," which is covered in a richly embroidered red silk decorated with Chinese mythological symbols.

Imperial wedding bed

Clocks and watches
Arguably the finest of the many and varied palace collections, the clocks and watches fill the Fengxian Pavilion in the southeastern corner of the eastern Inner Court. The size and creativity involved in some of the pieces – which are primarily European – is astonishing. One particularly inventive model has an automaton clad in European dress frantically writing eight Chinese characters on a scroll, which is being unrolled by two other mechanical figures.

Ornate carriage clock

Ceramics
In a ceramic salute to the Silk Road, several linked halls around the Inner Court display tomb figurines from the Sui (581–618) and Tang (618–906) dynasties. Still caked with earth, statues range from six inches to three feet (15 cm to 1m) in height, and depict overweight court ladies, Buddhas on elephants, and floppy-humped camels. A film offers some background on the pottery finds.

Empress Cixi
The Xianfu Pavilion is a memorial to the Empress Cixi's devious rise to power (see p23), as well as to the great lady's imperial extravagances, which so nearly crippled her country. Clothes, jewelry, embroidered socks, imported perfume, jade and ivory chopsticks, and pictures of clothes and food form the bulk of the exhibits. There are also examples of the empress's calligraphic skills in the form of painted wall hangings.

For more Beijing museums See pp42–3

🔟 Temple of Heaven

It was here that the emperor would make sacrifices and pray to heaven and his ancestors at the winter solstice. As the Son of Heaven, the emperor could intercede with the gods on behalf of his people and pray for a good harvest. Off-limits to the common people during the Ming and Qing dynasties, the temple complex is now fully open to the public and attracts thousands of visitors daily, including many local Chinese who come to enjoy the large and pleasant park in which the monuments are set.

Triple gate for emperor, officials, and gods

🄾 There are several small snack kiosks in the park grounds.

🄲 Just as fascinating as exploring the temple is observing the great numbers of Chinese who come to the park to dance, exercise, sing opera, play games of cards and mahjong, and fly kites.

Tian Tan Dong Lu (East Gate), Chongwen
• *Map F6*
• *6702 2617*
• *Subway: Chongwen Men or Qian Men*
• *Park open: 8am–6pm daily. Temple open: 8am–5pm*
• *Admission to temple: ¥30. Park free*

Top 10 Features

1. Hall of Prayer for Good Harvests
2. Painted Caisson Ceiling
3. Marble Platform
4. Red Step Bridge
5. Imperial Vault of Heaven
6. Echo Wall
7. Echo Stones
8. Round Altar
9. Hall of Abstinence
10. Temple of Heaven Park

1 Hall of Prayer for Good Harvests

Built in 1420, then rebuilt in 1889, this circular tower, with a conical roof of blue tiles and a gold finial, is the most beautiful building in Beijing *(right)*. One of the most striking facts about it is that it was constructed without the use of a single nail.

2 Painted Caisson Ceiling

The circular ceiling of the Hall of Prayer for Good Harvests has a gilded dragon and phoenix at its center *(below)*. The wood for the four central columns was imported from Oregon, as at the time China had no trees tall enough.

3 Marble Platform

The Hall of Prayer for Good Harvests sits atop three tiers of marble that form a circle 300 ft (90 m) in diameter and 20 ft (6 m) high *(above)*. The balusters on the upper tier are decorated with intricate dragon carvings that serve to signify the imperial nature of the structure.

For more on popular Chinese park activities See pp36–7

4 Red Step Bridge

A raised walkway of marble and stone that runs exactly along the north-south axis of the temple complex, the Red Step Bridge *(left)* connects the Hall of Prayer for Good Harvests with the Round Altar.

5 Imperial Vault of Heaven

A circular hall made of wood and capped by a conical roof, the Imperial Vault *(below)* once held the wooden spirit tablets that were used in the ceremonies that took place on the nearby Round Altar.

6 Echo Wall

The Imperial Vault is enclosed by the circular Echo Wall, which has the same sonic effects found in some European cathedrals, where even a whisper travels round to a listener on the other side.

7 Echo Stones

There are three rectangular stones at the foot of the staircase leading up to the Imperial Vault: stand on the first and clap to hear one echo; stand on the second stone and clap once for two echoes; clap once on the third for three echoes.

8 Round Altar

The altar is formed of marble slabs laid in nine concentric circles with each circle containing a multiple of nine pieces. The center of the altar *(right)* represents the center of the world and it is where the emperor carried out sacrifices.

Tian Tan

The Hall of Prayer for Good Harvests, or Qinian Dian, which is the iconic structure at the heart of the complex, is often incorrectly called the Temple of Heaven. There is, in fact, no single temple building and the name, which in Chinese is Tian Tan – a more literal translation of which is Altar of Heaven – refers to the whole complex.

9 Hall of Abstinence

A red-walled, compound surrounded by a moat spanned by decorative bridges, the Hall of Abstinence resembles a mini Forbidden City. This is where the emperor would spend the last 24 hours of his three-day fast prior to partaking in the Temple of Heaven ceremonies.

0 Temple of Heaven Park

Today, locals, lured both to the splendor of the buildings and to the crowds of tourists, use the extensive grounds to practice *tai ji quan (right)*, and other martial arts, and to exercise.

There are also ceremonial sacrificial altars at *Zhong Shan, Di Tan, and Ri Tan Parks* See p69, p81 & p87

TOP 10 Tian'an Men Square

Tian'an Men Guangchang (the Square of the Gate of Heavenly Peace) is not one of the world's most attractive public plazas. It also has unfortunate associations with death, in the physical form of Mao's Mausoleum and in the memories of the bloody climax of 1989's pro-democracy demonstrations. But it has witnessed triumphant events too, including the founding of the People's Republic of China, and it remains central to modern life in Beijing, surrounded by important national institutions and filled daily with visitors and kite flyers.

Mao's portrait still hangs from Tian'an Men

🍽 Cafés and restaurants ring the square, but there are better places a short walk south of Qian Men.

🕐 Mao's Mausoleum is best visited in the morning to avoid the afternoon queues.

Tian'an Men Square
• *Map L5*
• *Subway: Tian'an Men Xi, Tian'an Men Dong, or Qian Men*
• *China National Museum: 6512 8901. Open: Jul, Aug 8am–6pm daily. Sep–Jun 9am–4pm daily. Last admission 1 hr before closing. Admission: ¥30*
• *Mao's Mausoleum: 6513 2277. Open 8am–11.30am Tue–Sun. Free*
• *Qian Men: 6522 9382. Open 8:30am–4pm daily. Admission: ¥20*
• *Tian'an Men: 6524 3322. Open 8:30am–4:30pm daily. Admission: ¥10*

Top 10 Features

1 Tian'an Men
2 China National Museum
3 Mao's Mausoleum
4 Great Hall of the People
5 Monument to the Heroes
6 Qian Men
7 Arrow Tower
8 National Flag
9 Qian Men Old Railway Station
10 Bicycles

1 Tian'an Men

Mao proclaimed the founding of the People's Republic of China on October 1, 1949 from this massive Ming-dynasty gate *(above)*, where his huge portrait still hangs. The way to the Forbidden City is through here.

2 China National Museum

This brutal 1959 building on the eastern side of the square *(right)* combines the Museum of Chinese History and the Museum of the Revolution. Exhibits include stunning Chinese artistic masterpieces, as well as less impressive pieces of propaganda.

3 Mao's Mausoleum

In an imposing hall at the center of the square *(above)* lies the embalmed body of Mao, who died in 1976. Encased in a crystal casket and draped in a red flag, he is raised from his refrigerated chamber for twice-daily public viewings.

Great Hall of the People

A monolithic structure dominating the western side of the square, the Great Hall is the seat of the Chinese legislature. The vast auditorium and banqueting halls are open for part of every day except when the People's Congress is in session.

Monument to the Heroes

Erected in 1958, the granite monument *(left)* is decorated with bas-reliefs of episodes from the nation's revolutionary history and calligraphy from Communist veterans Mao Zedong and Zhou Enlai.

Qian Men

The "Front Gate", also known as Zhengyang Men ("Sun-facing Gate"), was constructed during the Ming dynasty and was the largest of the nine gates of the inner city wall. It now houses a city history museum.

Arrow Tower

With the Qian Men, the Arrow Gate *(above)* formed part of a great double gate. The walls that once flanked the gate were demolished in the 20th century.

City Walls

There were earlier defenses but it was during the Ming era (1368–1644) that the walls took on their recognizable shape of an outer wall with seven gates, and an inner wall with nine gates. Tragically, almost all was demolished in the 1950s and 1960s to make way for roads. The gates are remembered only in the names of the subway stations on the Second Ring Road.

National Flag

At the northern end of the square is a towering pole, from which flies the Chinese flag; a troop of People's Liberation Army (PLA) soldiers raises the flag each day at dawn and lowers it again at sunset.

Bicycles

Although car ownership in Beijing continues to rise dramatically, for the moment at least the bicycle remains the quintessentially Chinese way of getting around. Cyclists still crowd the wide avenues that ring Tian'an Men Square.

Qian Men Old Railway Station

The stripy building on the square's southeast corner is a British-built railway station. It now houses shops, an internet café, a branch of McDonald's, and a theater where performances of Beijing Opera take place.

For a look at the Tian'an Men area as it used to be, visit the Imperial City Museum See p68

15

TOP10 Lama Temple

Beijing's most spectacular place of worship is also the most famous Buddhist temple outside of Tibet. It has five main halls, each taller than the last, as well as some stunning statuary. The path through the Lama Temple proceeds from south to north – from earth to heaven.

1 Monks
At one time the were 1,500 monks at the temple, now there are only 70. Although of the same Yellow Hat sect as the Dalai Lama the monks are required to reject Tibetan independence.

Imperial dragon decoration

There are no refreshments available within the temple precincts, so if it's a hot day then remember to bring along your own bottle of water.

Photography is not allowed within the halls but you can take pictures of the exteriors and of the courtyards.

28 Yonghe Gong Dajie
• Map F1
• 6404 4499
• Subway: Yonghe Gong
• Open: Apr–Oct 9am–4.30pm daily. Nov–Mar 9am–4pm daily
• Admission: ¥25
• Audio guides are available for ¥20

Top 10 Features

1. Monks
2. Drum and Bell Towers
3. Hall of the Heavenly Kings
4. Hall of Eternal Harmony
5. Hall of Eternal Protection
6. Hall of the Wheel of Dharma
7. Hall of Ten Thousand Happinesses
8. Prayer Wheel
9. Incense Burner
10. Lion Statue

2 Drum and Bell Towers
The temple's Drum and Bell towers are in the first courtyard after passing through the main entrance. The huge bell has been removed from its tower and placed on the ground.

3 Hall of the Heavenly Kings
The first hall has a plump laughing Buddha, Milefo, back-to-back with Wei Tuo, the Guardian of Buddhist Doctrine. They are flanked by the Four Heavenly Kings.

4 Hall of Eternal Harmony
This, the second hall *(left)*, contains three manifestations of Buddha. These represent the past, present, and future, and are flanked by 18 *luohan* – those freed from the cycle of rebirth.

Hall of Eternal Protection

[Th]e third hall contains [Bu]ddhas of longevity and [me]dicine. It also has two [fam]ous *tangkas*, said to [ha]ve been embroidered [by] Emperor Qianlong's [mo]ther. Behind the hall [is a] bronze sculpture of [Mo]unt Meru, the center [of] the Buddhist universe.

6 Hall of the Wheel of Dharma

Hall four has a 20-foot (6-m) high statue of Tsongkhapa, the 14th-century founder of the Yellow Hat sect of Buddhism. Dominant in Tibetan politics for centuries, the sect is led by the Dalai Lama and Panchen Lama.

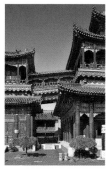

7 Hall of Ten Thousand Happinesses

The final pavilion *(left)* houses an 80-foot (25-m) high Buddha carved from a single piece of sandalwood. There's a splendid collection of Tibetan Buddhist objects in a room behind the hall.

8 Prayer Wheel

Spinning a prayer wheel *(right)* sends a prayer written on coiled paper to heaven. A little yellow arrow taped to the frame of the wheel reminds worshipers which direction (clockwise) to spin the wheel.

9 Incense Burner

There are incense burners in front of all the many altars throughout the temple. Shops lining the entryway to the complex and in the neighboring streets are piled with bundles of incense sticks for sale for use at the temple.

Panchen Lama

While the Dalai Lama, head of the sect to which the Lama Temple belongs, lives in exile, the second head, the Panchen Lama, resides in Beijing. In contrast to the Dalai Lama, the Panchen recognizes Chinese authority. However, the matter of the true identity of the Panchen Lama is a matter of controversy. China supports one candidate, while the Tibetans recognize another – only he vanished in suspicious circumstances in 1995.

Lion Statue

A large imperial lion *(right)* is a reminder that [the] complex was originally [the] residence of the man [wh]o would become Qing [Em]peror Yongzheng. On [asc]ending the throne in [17]22, and in keeping [wit]h tradition, his former [hom]e became a temple.

For more Beijing places of worship **See pp46–7**

🔟 Bei Hai Park

An imperial garden for more than a thousand years, Bei Hai was opened to the public in 1925. Filled with artificial hills, pavilions, and temples, it is associated with Kublai Khan, who redesigned it during the Mongol Yuan dynasty. These days, it is a fine place for a leisurely afternoon stroll, and perhaps a bit of boating on the lake.

Lakeside pavilions

Park gate

🍴 Aside from the famous Fangshan Restaurant, there are also small snack kiosks in the park.

🚪 There are four gates to the park: the most convenient is the south gate, close to the northwest corner of the Forbidden City; the north gate exits across the road from Hou Hai, where there are good eating and drinking options.

---

1 Wenjin Jie, Xicheng
• Map K1
• 6403 1102
• Subway: Tian'an Men Xi
• Open: Apr–Oct 6am–10pm daily. Nov–Mar 6:30am–9pm. All buildings close at 4pm year round
• Admission: Apr–Oct ¥10. Nov–Mar ¥5

Top 10 Features

1. Round City
2. Jade Island
3. White Dagoba
4. Yongan Temple
5. Fangshan Restaurant
6. Pavilion of Calligraphy
7. The Place of Serenity
8. Xiao Xitian Temple
9. Nine Dragon Screen
10. Zhong Nan Hai

Round City

Bei Hai was the site of Beijing's earliest imperial palace, although nothing remains other than a small pavilion on a site known as the Round City, and a large jade wine vessel said to have belonged to Kublai Khan.

Jade Island

Accessed by bridge from the south gate or by boat from the north gate, Bei Hai's willow-lined island *(right)* was created from the earth excavated to form the lake.

White Dagoba

Topping Jade Island, the 118-ft (36-m) high White Dagoba is a Tibetan-style stupa built to honor the visit of the fifth Dalai Lama in 1651. It has been rebuilt twice since.

Yongan Temple

Beneath the Dagoba the temple comprises a series of ascending halls including the Hall of the Wheel of Law with its central effigy of the Buddha Sakyamuni.

Fangshan Restaurant

Founded in 1926 by chefs of the imperial household, the restaurant *(left)* bases its menus on court cuisine. Standards have slipped but the lakeside setting still has great appeal.

Pavilion of Calligraphy

crescent-shaped hall Jade Island contains arly 500 stone tablets graved with the work famous Chinese ligraphers. If the hibits are less than thralling the walkways at lead to the pavilion e enchanting.

The Place of Serenity

In the northwest corner of the park is this beautiful garden *(left)*, created in the mid-18th century by the Qianlong emperor, with rockeries, pavilions, and ornate bridges over goldfish-filled pools.

Xiao Xitian Temple

Near the Place of Serenity is a trio of small temple buildings – the Pavilion of 10,000 Buddhas, the Glazed Pavilion, which is covered with green and yellow ceramic Buddhas, and the Xiao Xitian (Small Western Sky) Temple filled with fearsome-looking idols *(above)*.

Nine Dragon Screen

Bei Hai's most striking sight is an 89-ft (27-m) g, free-standing wall made of colorful glazed amic tiles and depicting nine intertwined dragons *elow)*. The Chinese dragon is a beneficent beast ering protection and good luck. The wall was signed to obstruct the passage of evil spirits, o are only able to travel in straight lines.

Zhong Nan Hai

Bei Hai means North Lake; the Middle (Zhong) and South (Nan) Lakes are part of an area occupied by China's political leaders and are off-limits to all except government officials. Zhong Nan Hai is regarded as the new Forbidden City.

Park play

Beijing's parks double as recreation centers, particularly for the city's elderly citizens. As soon as the parks open in the morning they gather to perform communal *tai ji quan* (tai chi) exercises. Many then spend the rest of the day in the park playing cards, dominos or mahjong, engaging in *yang ge* (fan dancing) or ballroom dancing, or simply reading the newspaper and talking with friends.

Hou Hai

The area around the joined lakes of Qian Hai and Hou Hai has traditionally been home to nobles and wealthy merchants. Several grand homes survive, hidden in the labyrinthine old lanes known as hutongs. This is a rare quarter of Beijing where the 21st century is kept at bay, and these back alleys represent one of the most satisfying parts of the city to explore on foot – or by rickshaw.

Al fresco dining at Qian Hai

Gaudy lamp shades for sale on Yandai Xie Jie

🍽 The Hou Hai area has several excellent restaurants and bars, see pp82–3.

🕐 Visit Hou Hai by day to explore the *hutongs* and historic residences, but do come back by night to dine and drink, and to see the lake glimmering with the flotilla of tea-candles that are floated out on the water each evening.

- Map D2
- Subway: Gulou Dajie
- Mansion of Prince Gong: 6616 8149. Open: Apr–Oct 7:30am–5:30pm. Nov–Mar 8:30am–4:30pm daily. Admission: ¥20
- Former Residence of Guo Moruo: 6612 5984. Open 9am–4.30pm Tue–Sun. Closed Dec 25 until 5th day of Chinese New Year. Admission: ¥20
- Song Qingling's Residence: 6616 8149. Open 9am–5:30pm Tue–Sun. Admission: ¥20

Top 10 Features

1. Lotus Lane
2. Boating and skating
3. Silver Ingot Bridge
4. Hutongs
5. Mansion of Prince Gong
6. Former Residence of Guo Moruo
7. Rickshaw tours
8. Song Qingling's Residence
9. Yandai Xie Jie
10. Drum and Bell Towers

Lotus Lane
This is the tourist-friendly name attached to the main lakeside parade of restaurants, bars, and cafés (including, inevitably, a Starbucks), many of which have attractive waterfront terraces.

Boating and skating
In summer the lakes are filled with small pedal boats, rented by the hour. By mid-December, they are frozen over *(above)* and a large area is corraled off for public ice-skating.

Silver Ingot Bridge
The narrow channel that connects Hou Hai's two lakes is spanned by the pretty, arched Silver Ingot Bridge *(right)*, which dates from the time of the Yuan dynasty (1279–1368).

Hutongs
The lakes lie at the heart of a sprawling old Beijing district, characterized by the traditional alleyways known as *hutongs*. These alleyways are lined for the most part by the blank outer walls of *siheyuan*, which are inward-looking houses that are arranged around a central courtyard. Each *siheyuan* houses several families.

Mansion of Prince Gong 5

Built for a Manchu official but seized by the imperial household, the former residence of Prince Gong is the best preserved historic mansion in Beijing. The garden is a pattern of corridors and pavilions, dotted with pools and gates *(right)*.

Former Residence of Guo Moruo 6

Beijing has countless "former residences of," mostly connected with Party favorites. Moruo was an author and influential figure in the rise of communism in China. His house offers the opportunity to see inside a *hutong* home.

Rickshaw tours 7

One way of seeing the *hutongs* is from a rickshaw. Prices and length of the tour are negotiable, but expect to pay around ¥180 per person for a two-hour jaunt with stop-offs at several place of interest.

Siheyuan

Traditional Beijing homes are arranged around a central courtyard. The main dwelling is on the north, with lesser halls on the other three sides. Originally homes of the well-to-do, over time many *siheyuan* were occupied by poorer families, who squeezed several households into the space formerly occupied by one. Modernization has destroyed many of these dwellings, but there is a movement to preserve those that have survived. A few have been converted into hotels *(see p116)*.

Drum and Bell Towers

Just north of the eastern end of Yandai Xie Jie these two imposing towers *(above)* once marked the northern-most limits of the city. You can ascend the towers for views of Hou Hai and beyond.

Song Qingling's Residence 8

Song Qingling was the wife of the revolutionary leader Sun Yat Sen. Her former living quarters are now a small museum (note the pistol that Sun Yat Sen gave his wife as a wedding present). The gardens surrounding the house are beautiful.

Yandai Xie Jie 9

One of the loveliest streets in Beijing is lined with historic buildings *(main pic)*, most of which have been converted into small boutiques and bars, including a temple that is now a café.

For more on Hou Hai and around **See pp78–83**

Summer Palace

A sprawling landscaped park on the edge of the city, the Summer Palace was a seasonal imperial retreat from the stifling confines of the Forbidden City. It was the favored haunt of the fiercesome Empress Cixi, who had it rebuilt twice: once following its destruction by French and English troops in 1860, and again in 1902, after it was plundered during the Boxer Rebellion.

Sea of Wisdom temple

Top 10 Features

1 Hall of Happiness and Longevity
2 Garden of Virtue and Harmony
3 Long Corridor
4 Longevity Hill
5 Tower of the Fragrance of the Buddha
6 Temple of the Sea of Wisdom
7 Marble Boat
8 Suzhou Street
9 South Lake Island
10 Seventeen-arch Bridge

Painted ceiling in the Long Corridor

○ There are several small snack kiosks in the park grounds.

✪ Avoid visiting on days with poor visibility when you risk missing the superb views across the lake that are one of the highlights of a visit to the Summer Palace.

6 miles (10 km) NW of central Beijing
• 6288 1144
• Subway: Xizhi Men then bus No. 32, or 808 from the zoo
• Open: Apr–Oct 6:30am–8pm daily. Nov–Mar 7am–7pm daily. Last admission 2 hrs before closing
• Admission: Apr–Oct ¥50. Nov–Mar ¥40
• Audio guides are available for ¥30

Hall of Happiness and Longevity
This impressive hall was the residence of the Empress Cixi. It has supposedly been left just as it was at the time of her death in 1908, complete with its Qing dynasty-era furniture.

Garden of Virtue and Harmony
This pretty complex of roofed corridors, small pavilions, rock gardens and pools also includes Cixi's private three-story theater *(left)*. The buildings now contain Qing-era artifacts, from vehicles to costumes and glassware.

Long Corridor
From the Garden of Virtue and Harmony the aptly named Long Corridor zigzags along the shore of the lake, interrupted along its length by four pavilions. The ceilings and beams of this corridor are decorated with over 14,000 scenic paintings.

It is possible to get out to the Summer Palace by boat on the old canal system **See p106**

Longevity Hill
At around the half-
way point of the Long
Corridor a series of
buildings ascends the
slopes of artificially
created Longevity Hill
(below). The start of the
sequence is marked at
the lakeside by a very
fine decorative gate, or
pailou.

Tower of the Fragrance of the Buddha
Toward the peak of
Longevity Hill rises this
prominent octagonal
tower. The stiff climb
is rewarded with views
from the balcony over
the yellow roofs of the
halls and pavilions to
the lake below.

Temple of the Sea of Wisdom
North of the Fragrance
of the Buddha tower is
a green- and yellow-tiled
temple decorated with
glazed Buddhist effigies,
many of which have
sadly been vandalized.

Marble Boat
Cixi paid for this
extravagant folly (above)
with funds meant for
the modernization of the
Imperial Navy. The super-
structure of the boat is
made of wood painted
white to look like marble.
Boat trips to South Lake
Island depart from a
neighboring jetty.

Suzhou Street
At the foot of
Longevity Hill on its
north side is Suzhou
Street, a shopping
street built for the
amusement of the
Qianlong emperor,
his concubines and
eunuchs, who would play
at being shoppers,
shopkeepers, and
pickpockets.

Seventeen-arch Bridge
South Lake Island is
connected to the eastern
shore by an elegant bridge
(above) with a marble
lion crowning each of the
544 balusters along its
length, all supposedly
individual. A large bronze
ox, dating back to 1755
but looking entirely
modern, reposes on
the eastern shore.

South Lake Island
Crowning this small
island on the south side
of Kunming Lake is the
Dragon King Temple
(Longwang Miao), which
is dedicated to the god
of rivers, seas, and rain.

Empress Cixi
Cixi is remembered as
one of China's most
powerful women.
Having borne one
emperor's son as an
imperial concubine, she
became the power
behind the throne to
two more: her son and
her nephew. When she
blocked state reforms
and lent support to the
xenophobic Boxers in
their rebellion, she
unwittingly paved the
way for the end of
the imperial era.

For more parks and gardens **See p37**

798 Art District

Since the first artists set up in Da Shan Zi's newly-vacated 798 factory in 2001, the East German-built industrial compound has become a world-famous center of contemporary Chinese art. Alongside the studios and galleries, there are also chic cafés, bars, and restaurants, and a growing number of small designer shops and showrooms. The area is popular with Chinese tourists, who arrive by the coach-load at weekends.

798 factory

Grafitti-daubed wall in the factory compound

⊙ Besides AT Café another good dining option is Vincent's, which specializes in Breton-style buckwheat crêpes. It is located just around the corner from the China Art Seasons gallery.

⊙ Most galleries are open from around 11am to 7pm, closed on Mondays.

2–4 Jiu Xian Qiao Lu, Chaoyang district, northeast of the Holiday Inn Lido complex

Top 10 Features

1. 798 Space
2. Maoist grafitti
3. AT Café
4. China Art Seasons
5. White Space
6. Timezone 8
7. Tianzi
8. Public sculpture
9. South Gate Space
10. 798 Photo Gallery

798 Space
The first gallery to open in Da Shan Zi, 798 Space *(above)* remains at the heart of the district. It is worth visiting for the spectacle of the cavernous main hall with its curious multiple-arched roof.

Maoist grafitti
When many of the abandoned factory spaces were being converted for use as galleries, the artists instructed the decorators to leave untouched the giant Maoist slogans that had been lettered on the walls by the former workers – as at 798 Space *(left)*. "Mao Zedong is the red star in our hearts," reads one.

AT Café
A fashionable café whose notable feature is a bare-brick dividing wall punctured by massive holes, AT *(left)* serves as the unofficial canteen for the artists and gallery staff who work in the area.

Every April/May the 798 Art District plays host to the annual Da Shan Zi Art Festival **See p35**

China Art Seasons

Of 798's very many galleries, most of which change their exhibitions on a monthly basis, this place consistently presents some of the most worthwhile work. It represents top artists like Xiao Long, whose series "Intellectual Youth" (below) showed here.

White Space

Foreign art dealers are already present in numbers in 798. The striking White Space (left) was one of the first such galleries, a branch of the Berlin-based Alexander Ochs Gallery.

Timezone 8

Established in 2001 by Texan Robert Bernell, Timezone 8 (below), which occupies a former factory canteen, is Beijing's best art bookshop. It also incorporates a gallery that specializes in photographic art.

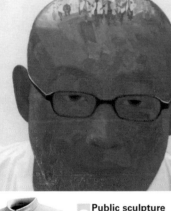

Tianzi

Feng Ling is a young fashion designer whose work is displayed at her boutique, Tianzi, in the same building as White Space. Her clothes are Sino Pop Art, and include items such as elegant linen tunics printed with a phrase from a Mao Zedong poem.

Public sculpture

Throughout the 798 compound large pieces of sculpture stand beside the lanes and pathways, and in courtyards. They are "in storage," like this giant Mao tunic (left) outside a local media headquarters, awaiting proper homes or buyers.

798 Photo Gallery

In addition to often excellent and regularly changing exhibitions of work by both Chinese and foreign photographers, the gallery also has a couple of mezzanine levels where a selection of photographic prints for sale are displayed.

South Gate Space

Not a gallery, the South Gate is an exciting, small performance space, used for theater, dance, and music. It fills the gap between club and full-scale theater auditorium, and is a favorite with visiting international acts. Check the local English-language free press to find out what's on.

Brave new worlds

1985 marks the arrival of the avant garde in Chinese art. This is the year that controversial student graduation shows ignited intense debate in artistic circles. The following year saw the first dabblings with performance art, and a New York City gallery introduced the new Chinese art to an international audience.

For more Beijing galleries to visit **See p49**

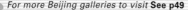

25

Ming Tombs

The resting place for 13 of the 16 Ming-dynasty (1368–1644) emperors, this is China's finest example of imperial funerary architecture. The site was selected because of its auspicious feng shui alignment; a ridge of mountains to the north cradles the tombs on three sides, protecting the dead from the evil spirits carried on the north wind. The tombs are spread over 15 square miles (40 sq km). Three (Chang Ling, Ding Ling, and Zhao Ling) have been restored and are always busy. Unrestored, the rest are open but quiet.

The Great Palace Gate, leading to the Spirit Way

🍴 There are snack kiosks at the site.

🔷 The Ming Tombs are most conveniently seen as part of a trip to the Great Wall at Badaling. Many hotels arrange tours for less than ¥100. The government operated Tour Bus 2 leaves regularly for the tombs and wall from just east of Qian Men on Tian'an Men Square every day from 6:30am onwards; the fare is ¥50 per person.

---

30 miles (45 km) NW of Beijing
• 6076 1423
• Bus 845 from Xizhi Men (near subway) to Zhengfa Daxue in Changping, then a taxi or bus 314 to Da Gong Men
• Open: Apr–Oct 8am–5:30pm daily. Nov–Mar 8:30am–5pm
• Admission: Spirit Way ¥30. Chang Ling ¥45. Ding Ling ¥60. Zhao Ling ¥30

Top 10 Features

1. Memorial Arch
2. Stele Pavilion
3. Spirit Way
4. Chang Ling Tomb
5. Hall of Eminent Favor
6. Ding Ling Treasures
7. Spirit Tower
8. Ding Ling Tomb
9. Ding Ling Burial Chamber
10. Zhao Ling Tomb

1 Memorial Arch

Marking the entrance to the site is a magnificent five-arched gate *(below)*, built of white marble, and erected in 1540. At 40 ft (12 m) high and more than 92 ft (28 m) wide, it is the largest of its kind in China, and boasts beautiful bas-relief carvings.

2 Stele Pavilion

After the Memorial Arch the road passes through the Great Palace Gate and the tunnel-like arch of the Stele Pavilion. Here the largest stele in China projects from the shell of a giant *bixi* (dragon-tortoise) and bears the names of the emperors buried at the site.

3 Spirit Way

Part of the 4-mile (7-km) approach to the tombs, the Spirit Way *(above)* is lined with 18 pairs of giant guardians – stone statues of court officials, imperial warriors, animals, and mythical Chinese beasts.

4 Chang Ling Tomb

The resting place of the Yongle emperor *(left)*, the builder of the Forbidden City and Temple of Heaven, is the oldest and grandest tomb. It has been well restored, but the chamber where Yongle, his wife, and 16 concubines are buried has never been excavated.

5 Hall of Eminent Favor

One of China's most impressive surviving Ming buildings, this double-eaved sacrificial hall is the centerpiece of the Chang Ling tomb complex. It stands on a triple-tiered marble terrace and 32 gigantic cedar columns *(left)* support the roof.

3 Ding Ling Tomb

This is the tomb of the longest-reigning Ming ruler, the emperor Wanli (1573–1620). His profligate life began the downfall of the dynasty. Building his tomb involved 30,000 workers and took six years to complete.

7 Spirit Tower

Rising up from the third courtyard of the Chang Ling complex, the tower marks the entrance to the burial chamber. This takes the form of an earthen tumulus girdled by a wall half a mile (1 km) in circumference.

6 Ding Ling Treasures

In addition to an impressive statue of the Yongle emperor, the Hall of Eminent Favor also contains artifacts from the Wanli emperor's tomb (the Ding Ling). These include a crown of golden wire topped by two dragons *(above)*.

The Ming dynasty

The 276-year Ming ("brilliant") dynasty rule was one of the longest and most stable periods in Chinese history. The founder of the Ming rose from humble beginnings via military successes to become emperor. He was succeeded by his grandson, who, in turn was succeeded by his son, who proclaimed himself emperor Yongle ("Eternal Joy"). It was Yongle who moved the capital from Nanjing to Beijing where he created a new city.

9 Ding Ling Burial Chamber

This is the only burial chamber to be excavated and opened to the public. Visitors descend to a central throne room and a rear annex with three red-lacquer coffins *(left)*, belonging to Wanli and his two wives.

Zhao Ling Tomb

The resting place of the 13th Ming emperor, Longqing (1537–72), who gained the throne at the age of 30 and died six years later. It has an attractive triple-bridge over a stream.

For more daytrips out of Beijing **See pp98–101**

TOP 10 Great Wall of China

The Great Wall snakes through the countryside over deserts, hills, and plains for several thousand miles. At its closest point it is less than 40 miles (60 km) from Beijing. The wall was created following the unification of China under Qin Shi Huangdi (221–210 BC). Despite impressive battlements, it ultimately proved ineffective; it was breached in the 13th century by the Mongols and again, in the 17th century, by the Manchus. Today, only select sections of its crumbling remains have been fully restored, with four main sites accessible from Beijing: Badaling, Mutianyu, Huanghua Cheng, and Simatai.

Souvenir stall at Badaling

🌀 The wall is exposed to the elements: it is extremely hot in summer (bring sun cream and lots of water) and bitterly cold in winter.

🍴 There are cafés and refreshment stands at each of the main four sites, although it's better to bring your own food.

Badaling *44 miles (70 km) NW of Beijing • 6912 2222 • Bus 1 from Qian Men • Open 7:30am–5pm daily • ¥45*

Mutianyu *56 miles (90 km) N of Beijing • 6162 6505 • Bus 6 from Xuanwu Men • Open 7am–6:30pm daily • ¥35*

Huanghua Cheng *37 miles (60 km) N of Beijing • Open 8am–5pm Mon–Fri; 7:30am–5:30pm Sat, Sun • ¥25*

Simatai *68 miles (110 km) NE of Beijing • 6903 1051 • Bus 6 from Xuanwu Men • Open 8am–5pm daily • ¥40*

Top 10 Features

1. Badaling
2. Great Wall Museum
3. Juyong Guan
4. Commune at the Great Wall
5. Mutianyu
6. Huanghua Cheng
7. Simatai
8. Jingshanling
9. Gubeikou
10. Shanhaiguan

Badaling

The restored Ming fortification at Badaling *(below)* is the closest section of the wall to Beijing. Although perpetually busy, it is possible to escape the crowds by walking along the wall; and the views are spectacular.

Great Wall Museum

Housed in an imitation Qing dynasty building at Badaling, the museum presents the history of the region from neolithic times, as well as detailing the construction of the wall. Admission is covered in the cost of your wall ticket.

Juyong Guan

This pass is on the way to Badaling. With unscalable mountains on either side it is easy to see why the spot was chosen for defence. Early cannons remain on the ramparts *(below)*. Also worth seeing are Buddhist carvings on a stone platform, or "cloud terrace," in the middle of the pass.

Commune at the Great Wall

Within sight of the wall at Badaling, the Commune (right) consists of 12 stunning, contemporary villas, each designed by a different, celebrated Asian architect. The complex operates as a hotel (see p113), but non-guests can drop by the restaurant for lunch.

Mutianyu

The appeal of Mutianyu lies in its dramatic hilly setting and less intrusive tourist industry. With a series of watchtowers along its restored length, the wall here dates from 1368.

Huanghua Cheng

On the same stretch of wall as Mutianyu, Huanghua Cheng (below) is an exhilarating section of Ming fortifications that is far less developed than most other parts. The great barrier is split into two by a large reservoir. The crumbling masonry can be uneven and fairly treacherous, so you need to take care.

Gubeikou

Lying farther west of Jingshanling, Gubeikou is a heavily fortified pass from where you can begin a 15-mile (25-km) walk to Simatai. It is, if you are really fit, possible to do it in one day.

Shanhaiguan

This is where the wall ends (or begins), at the sea. East of town, the "First Pass Under Heaven" is a formidable section of wall attached to a gatehouse. It lies some 218 miles (350 km) east of Beijing but it does make for a worthwhile overnight trip.

Simatai

The wall at Simatai (above) has only been partially repaired, and so affords a more genuine impression of the original wall. It is very steep and hazardous here in parts, and can even be quite risky to navigate.

Jingshanling

The starting point for a 6-mile (10-km) trek to Simatai, which because of the steep and stony trail usually takes around four hours. The views as the wall winds over sharp peak after sharp peak are fantastic, but you have to work for them.

Visiting the wall

Most hotels are able to organize a trip to the wall, usually combined with a visit to the Ming Tombs (see pp26–7). However, be sure to find out whether there are any unwanted diversions planned to cloisonné workshops, jade factories, or Chinese medicine clinics. Small groups can have a more personalized visit, and see the more remote parts of the wall, by hiring a taxi for the day from Beijing and sharing the cost.

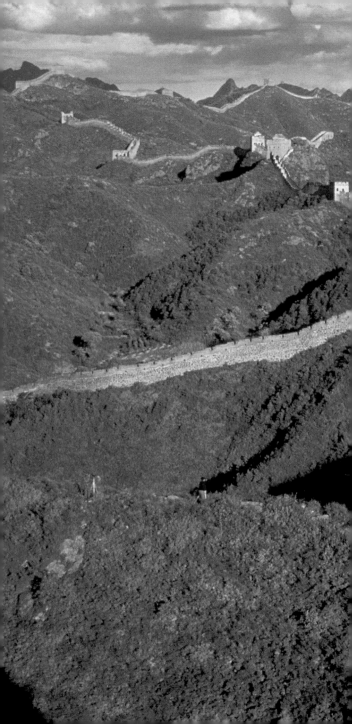

Left **Mongol horsemen** Center **Empress Cixi** Right **Red Army tank**

TOP 10 Moments in History

1 500,000 BC: Peking Man hunts and gathers
Unearthed in the 1920s from a cave at Zhoukoudian, 30 miles (45 km) SW of Beijing, 40-odd fossilized bones and primitive implements were identified as the prehistoric remains of Peking Man *(Homo erectus Pekinensis)*, who lived in the vicinity over 500,000 years ago.

2 1215: Genghis Khan sacks Zhongdu
The future Beijing was developed as an auxiliary capital under the Liao (907–1125) and Jin dynasties (1115–1234), at which time it was known as Zhongdu. In 1215 it was invaded and razed by a Mongol army led by the fearsome Genghis Khan.

"Last Emperor" Pu Yi

3 Late 13th century: Marco Polo visits
Under the first emperor of the Mongol Yuan dynasty, Kublai Khan (r. 1260–1294), the city became known as Khanbalik, and was one of twin capitals – the other was Yuanshangdu, or Xanadu – of the largest empire ever known. The Italian traveler Marco Polo was dazzled by the imperial palace: "The building is altogether so vast and beautiful, that no man on earth could design anything superior to it."

4 1403–25: Construction of the Forbidden City
The Ming emperor Yongle (r. 1403–24) destroyed the palaces of his Mongol predecessors in order to rebuild the city, which he renamed Beijing (Northern Capital). He is credited with laying the foundations for the city as it is today, and the Forbidden City and Temple of Heaven began to take shape during his reign.

5 1900: Boxer Rebellion
Western powers, frustrated by the reluctance of the Chinese to open up to foreign trade, put the imperial court under pressure, eventually going to war to protect their trade in opium. In 1900, championed by the Empress Cixi, a band of rebels from north China known as the Boxers attacked Beijing's Foreign Legation Quarter. A joint eight-nation army had to be sent to lift the siege.

6 1912: The End of Empire
The last emperor, Pu Yi, ascended the throne at the age of three. Four years later, in February 1912, his brief reign was brought to a premature end when he was forced to abdicate by general Yuan Shikai's new National Assembly.

Previous pages **Great Wall north of Beijing**

7 1949: Founding of the People's Republic of China

On January 31, 1949, Communist forces led by Mao Zedong seized Beijing. On October 1, Mao proclaimed the foundation of the People's Republic of China from the gallery of the Tian'an Men.

8 1965: Launch of the Cultural Revolution

Having socialized industry and agriculture, Mao called on the masses to transform society itself. All distinctions between manual and intellectual work were to be abolished and class distinction was to be eradicated. The revolution reached its violent peak in 1967, with the Red Guards spreading fear and havoc.

9 1976: The death of Mao

On September 9, 1976 Mao died. The destructive policies of the Cultural Revolution were abandoned. Mao's long-time opponent Deng Xiaoping emerged as leader, implementing reforms that encouraged greater economic freedom.

10 2001: Beijing is awarded the 2008 Olympics

In July 2001 International Olympic Committee members meeting in Moscow awarded China the 2008 Games. Thousands flocked to Tian'an Men Square to celebrate – the first unscripted mass gathering there since 1989's massacre.

Tian'an Men, birthplace of modern China

Top 10 Chinese Inventions

1 Porcelain
The Chinese invented porcelain a thousand years before Europe caught on – and kept production methods secret to protect their competitive advantage.

2 Printing
In the 11th century, the Chinese carved individual characters on pieces of clay, inventing movable block type.

3 Paper money
Developed by Chinese merchants as certificates of exchange. Lighter than coins, bills were soon adopted by the government.

4 Gunpowder
Stumbled on by Daoist alchemists seeking the elixir of life.

5 Seismometer
A ball fell from one of four dragon's mouths to indicate the direction of the quake.

6 Abacus
Invented during the Yuan dynasty and still in use throughout China today.

7 Magnetic compass
Developed from an instrument used for *feng shui* and geomancy, it helped the Chinese explore the world.

8 Paper
A prototype paper was made from mulberry bark, although bamboo, hemp, linen, and silk were also used to write on.

9 Crossbow
Better range, accuracy, and penetration than the standard bow.

10 Decimal system
Developed alongside the writing system and led to mathematical advances.

The Science and Technology Museum includes an exhibition of Chinese inventions **See p96**

Left **Mooncake** Center **Lantern Festival** Right **Dragon Boat Festival**

Festivals and Events

Chinese New Year

Also known as Spring Festival, Beijing's favorite holiday is celebrated with a cacophony of fireworks, let off night and day across the city. There are also temple fairs with stilt-walkers, acrobats, and fortune-tellers. Everyone who can heads for their family home, where gifts are exchanged and children are kept quiet with red envelopes stuffed with cash so adults can watch the annual Spring Festival Gala on national television. ⏱ *Three days from the first day of the first moon, usually late Jan or early Feb*

Lantern Festival

Coinciding with a full moon, this festival marks the end of the 15-day Spring Festival celebrations. Lanterns bearing auspicious characters or in the shape of animals are hung everywhere. It is also a time for eating the sticky rice balls known as *yuanxiaio*. ⏱ *The 15th day of the lunar calendar (end of Feb)*

Tomb-Sweeping Festival

Also known as Qing Ming, which literally means "clear and bright." Chinese families visit their ancestors' graves to tidy them up and make offerings of snacks and alcohol, an event that often turns into a picnic. ⏱ *Apr 5, but Apr 4 in leap years*

International Labor Day

A reminder that China is still a Communist nation, Labor Day is celebrated with a week-long holiday, which marks the start of the domestic travel season. Shops, offices, and other businesses close for at least three days, and often for the whole week. Don't plan on doing any out-of-town travel during this time. ⏱ *May 1*

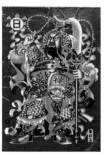

Guardian hung on doors to welcome Chinese New Year

Dragon Boat Festival (Duanwu Jie)

Drums thunder and paddles churn up the water as dragon-headed craft compete for top honors. The festival remembers the honest official, Qu Yuan, who, the story goes, drowned himself 2,500 years ago after banishment from the court of the Duke of Chu. Shocked citizens threw rice cakes into the water to distract the fish from nibbling on his body, hence the wholesale consumption of these delicacies on this date every year. ⏱ *The 5th day of the 5th lunar month (early Jun)*

Mid-Autumn Festival

Also known as the Harvest or Moon Festival, this is traditionally a time for family reunions and for giving boxes of sweet and savory mooncakes (*yuebing*). ⏱ *The 15th day of the 8th lunar month (usually Sep)*

Cricket-fighting

Cricket season in Beijing is nothing to do with the genteel English game. The Chinese version involves ruthless antennae-on-antennae action as cricket-fanciers goad their insects into battle in the plastic bowls that serve as gladiatorial arenas. Once the favorite sport of emperors it now takes place in backstreets all over town. *Mid-Sep to the end of Oct*

National Day

Marking the anniversary of Mao's 1949 speech in which he declared the foundation of the People's Republic. Crowds turn out to watch massed parades of high-kicking soldiers, and a jam-packed Tian'an Men Square is colored red by a sea of hand-held, waving flags. ◈ *Oct 1*

Christmas Day

Not a traditional Chinese holiday but the festivities have been adopted via Hong Kong, which means that there is a stress on the commercial aspect. High-street stores are bedecked with *Shengdan Laoren*, the Chinese version of Father Christmas. ◈ *Dec 25*

New Year's Day

Although overshadowed by Chinese New Year, which takes place soon after, Western New Year is still a public holiday throughout China. ◈ *Jan 1*

National Day parade

Top 10 Annual Cultural Events

1 Meet In Beijing
Performance festival with an unpredictable mix of Chinese and foreign theater acts. ◈ *Various venues • May*

2 Da Shan Zi Art Festival
Not so much an art festival as an arts circus, incorporating music, dance, and performance. ◈ *798 Art District • Late Apr–mid-May*

3 Midi Music Festival
Four days of home-grown punk, metal, rock, and dance. Venues and dates change from year to year. ◈ *May*

4 Beijing Bienniale
Artists from a multitude of countries exhibit beside their Chinese counterparts. ◈ *National Art Museum • Odd years, late Sep–late Oct*

5 Beijing Music Festival
Month-long extravaganza of local and international soloists and orchestras. ◈ *Various venues • Oct*

6 Beijing Pop Festival
International name acts supported by local talent. ◈ *Chaoyang Park • Sep*

7 Beijing Book Fair
Three days for the trade followed by two days of public participation. ◈ *Chaoyang Park • 1st weekend of Sep*

8 Beijing Art Fair
Almost 100 galleries from around the globe in Beijing to sell, sell, sell. ◈ *Mid-Apr*

9 Chaoyang Festival
Street theater, live music, circus, and dance. ◈ *Chaoyang Park • Late Jan, early Feb*

10 Beijing International Theater Festival
A month of musicals, operas, puppet shows and dramas. ◈ *Various venues • May*

Left **Outdoor drummers** Center **Bird fancying** Right **Kite flying**

🔟 Outdoor Activities

Kite flying
A major hobby among gents of all ages, especially popular on public holidays when the skies above the city's parks and squares are crowded with fluttering birds, dragons, lions, and laughing Buddhas.

Mahjong
Like gin rummy it's all about collecting sets or runs to score points, only mahjong uses tiles, not playing cards. A visit to any Beijing park will invariably be soundtracked by the rat-a-tat of slammed pieces.

Water calligraphy

Street dancing
Ballroom dancing is hugely popular with the elderly, but in Beijing it doesn't take place in ballrooms but out on the street. On warm evenings, car parks and sidewalks are filled with dancers congregated around a boombox. At the Workers' Stadium you can get up to four different groups on the forecourt in front of the north gate – choose your style: waltz, polka, foxtrot, or gavotte.

Jianzi
Western kids play it with a football, passing the ball around with head, knees, and feet, the idea being not to let it touch the ground; the Chinese have their own version playing with what resembles a large plastic shuttlecock. It's called *jianzi* and it is something of a national obsession, played by young and old alike, male and female.

Tai chi
Looking to improve the flow of *qi* (life force) through their bodies, early each morning crowds of mostly elderly people gather in Beijing's parks to indulge in mass movements of *tai chi*, or *tai ji quan* as it's better known in China. Although the discipline has its origins in martial arts, for most folks it's more about making sure that the joints don't seize up.

Yang Ge
Dancing accessorized with brightly-colored, silk fans (an art known as *yang ge*) is popular with middle-aged ladies. It incorporates stylized movements derived from folk dancing.

Ballroom dancing Beijing style

...nging opera down at the park

Bird fancying
The Chinese have never ...een great keepers of pets, ...rtly because Mao outlawed ...as a bourgeois practice. The ...ception has been the keeping ... caged songbirds, which is a ...ne-honored hobby. The birds ...e often taken to the park by ...eir owners and hung in the ...ees to provide a sweet ...oundtrack to casual socializing.

Water calligraphy
Using a mop-like brush and ...bowl of plain water, characters ...e painted on the sidewalk. ...nce dry, the characters ...sappear. It is supposed to ...ercise the mind and body. ...ssing coins into the bowl ...ll not be appreciated.

Opera singing
The Chinese are rarely ...hibited by self-consciousness ...d behave in public as they ...ould at home. Hence, parks ...e for singing. They gather in ...oups, taking it in turns to ...rform for each other; favored ...aces for this are on the north ...ore of the lake at Bei Hai and ... the Temple of Heaven park.

Qigong
Qigong combines breathing ...ercises, movement and ...editation to positively channel ...dy energy, or *qi*. Its adherents ...aim that regular practice can ...event illness and reduce stress.

Top 10 Parks

1 Bei Hai Park
Classic ornamental gardens with a large lake for boating (*see pp18–19*).

2 Chaoyang Park
The largest afforested park in Beijing, with well-maintained flower and grass areas. ⊗ Subway: *Dong Si Shi Tiao, then taxi*

3 Di Tan Park
Large green spaces and cypress trees, and the striking Temple of Earth (*see p81*).

4 Xiang Shan Park
An hour's drive northwest of the center but worth it for thickly wooded slopes dotted with pavilions (*see p95*).

5 Grand View Garden
A park created for a hit TV series complete with pavilions, lake, and zigzag bridge. ⊗ *Map C6 • Subway: Changchun Jie, then taxi*

6 Jing Shan Park
A hilly park with a pavilion providing views of the roofscape of the Forbidden City to the south (*see p68*).

7 Long Tan Park
Lots of lakes, a kid's amusement park, and an enchanting water-screen show. ⊗ *Map G6 • Subway: Chongwen Men, then taxi*

8 Ri Tan Park
One of Beijing's oldest parks, with an altar for imperial sacrifice (*see p85*).

9 Temple of Heaven Park
Historic structures and a vast expanse of well-tended gardens, including a rose garden (*see pp12–13*).

10 Zhong Shan Park
Just outside the walls of the Forbidden City, Zhong Shan offers a respite from the crowds (*see p69*).

For activities for children **See pp52–3**

Left **Beijing Opera cast** Right **Acrobats**

🔟 Beijing Opera

1 Colors
The colors of the performers' painted faces symbolize the individual characters' qualities. Red, for example, represents loyalty and courage. Purple stands for solemnity and a sense of justice, green for bravery and irascibility.

Painted face

2 Acrobatics
Beijing Opera is a form of "total theater" with singing, speech, mime, and acrobatics that combine graceful gymnastics and movements from the martial arts. Training is notoriously hard. Costumes are designed to make the jumps seem more spectacular by billowing out as they spin.

3 Musical instruments
Despite the dramatic visual elements of Beijing Opera, the Chinese say that they go to "listen" to opera, not to see it. Typically six or seven musicians accompany the dramatics. The stringed instruments usually include the *erhu*, or Chinese two-stringed violin, while percussion includes instruments such as clappers, gongs, and drums.

4 Sheng
There are four main role types in Beijing Opera: *sheng* (male), *dan* (female), *jing* (painted face), and *chou* (clown). *Sheng* are divided into *laosheng*, who wear beards and represent old men, *xiaosheng* who are young men, and *wusheng*, who are the acrobats and whose roles are typically those of warriors.

5 Dan
Dan are the female roles. *Laodan* are old ladies and *caidan* the female comedians, while *wudan* are the martial artists. The most important category, *qingyi*, usually play respectable and decent ladies in elegant costumes.

6 Jing
Jing have stylized patterned colored faces, and represent warriors, heroes, statesmen, adventurers, and demons. Not only are these characters the

host striking looking but they also usually have the most forceful personalities.

Chou

The *chou* are the comic characters and they're denoted by white patches on their noses. Patches of different shape and size mean roles of different character. It is the *chou* who keep the audience laughing.

Mei Lanfang

Mei Lanfang was the premost male interpreter of the female role *(dan)* during Beijing Opera's heyday in the 1920s and 1930s. Traditionally all female roles were played by male actors, although no longer.

Repertoire

The traditional repertoire includes more than 1,000 works, mostly based on popular tales. Modern productions aimed at tourists often include English-language displays of the text.

Monkey

Clever, resourceful, and brave, Monkey is one of the favorite characters in Beijing Opera. He has his origins in classic Chinese literature.

an (left),
hou (center),
onkey (right)

Top 10 Beijing Opera Venues

1 Beijing Traditional Opera Theater
Highlights shows in English.
◈ 8 Majiapu Dong Lu, south of Taoranting Park • 6756 2287

2 Chang'an Grand Theater
Daily two-hour performances of mostly complete operas.
◈ 7 Jianguo Men Nei Dajie
• Map G4 • 6510 1308

3 Chaoyang Theater
Daily hour-long performances of highlights.
◈ 36 Dongsanhuan Bei Lu
• Map H3 • 6507 2421

4 East Pioneer Theater
Occasional two-hour highlights shows. ◈ 8-2 Dongdan 3 Tiao, off Wangfujing Dajie • Map N4 • 6559 7394

5 Hu Guang Hui Guan
Daily one-hour highlights shows. ◈ 13 Hufang Lu • Map D5 • 6351 8284

6 Lao She Teahouse
Daily 90-minute variety shows that include Beijing Opera. ◈ 3 Qian Men Xi Dajie
• Map L6 • 6303 6830

7 Li Yuan Theater
Daily 80-minute highlights shows. ◈ Qian Men Hotel, 175 Yong'an Lu • Map D6 • 8315 7297

8 Mansion of Prince Gong
Summer performances only (see p21). ◈ 17 Qianhai Xi Jio
• Map D2 • 6616 8149

9 Tian Qiao Happy Teahouse
Old Beijing variety shows Mon–Fri. ◈ 1 Bei Wei Lu • Map E6 • 6304 0617

10 Zheng Yi Temple Theater
Daily two-hour performances.
◈ 220 Xiheyan Qian Men
• Map K6 • 8315 1649

For more on entertainment in Beijing **See pp54–5**

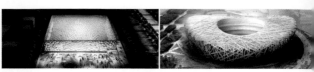

Left **National Aquatics Center** Right **National Olympic Stadium**

Beijing Olympics 2008

1 CCTV Building
Of all the buildings under construction in preparation for the Olympics, the most striking is the new headquarters of China Central Television. Designed by Dutch architect Rem Koolhaas, it is a gravity-defying loop of horizontal and vertical sections. When completed it's likely to become one of the world's most recognizable icons. 🕲 Map H4

2 New International Terminal, Beijing Airport
The largest construction project on earth, British architect Sir Norman Foster's new terminal will welcome athletes from around the world to the 29th Olympiad in 2008. The design resembles a soaring dragon in red and yellow.

3 National Olympic Stadium
Set to be the centerpiece of the Olympics, when finished Beijing's new stadium will be the world's biggest enclosed space, capable of holding 100,000 spectators. The innovative design by Swiss architects Herzog and de Meuron resembles a giant bird's nest.

4 National Aquatics Center
The "Water Cube" is a complex of five pools intended to stage the Olympic swimming and diving events. It's another ground-breaking design, in this case inspired by the formation of bubbles and molecules.

5 National Grand Theater
French architect Paul Andreu's silvery "Giant Egg" *(see p67)*, completed in 2006, provides a shocking contrast to the monolithic, slab-like Socialist architecture of neighboring Tian'an Men Square. The building is surrounded by a reflective moat and accessed by an underwater tunnel (upsetting Chinese critics who claim this resembles the entrance to a traditional tomb). At night, a part of the façade is transparent so passers-by can see what's going on inside. 🕲 Map K5

6 National Indoor Stadium
Built to host gymnastics and handball during the 2008 Games, the stadium boasts a sinuously curving roof with slatted beams, which is inspired by traditional Chinese folding fans. After the Games are over, the stadium will stage entertainment events, such as concerts.

CCTV Building

Olympic Green Convention Center

e Convention Center is one
the principal buildings of the
in Olympic Green complex in
e north of the city. It will serve
the competition venue for
e fencing events. It will also
uble as the main press center
the Games.

Beijing Books Building

China's conservative state-
ned Xinhua bookstore teamed
with maverick Dutch architect
m Koolhaas to produce one
the world's most digitally
namic structures. The entire
nt wall of the eight-story
ilding will be one vast
ectronic bookshelf" with a
nt video screen, which will
dress passing pedestrians
ich like the talking billboards
the movie *Bladerunner*.

Television Cultural Center

m Koolhaas's third high-profile
ijing project is a companion
ce to his show-stopping CCTV
ilding. It may lack the visual
pact of its sibling but when
mplete it will have much to
er Beijingers and visitors to
e city, combining as it does
lanned five-star hotel and
)0-seat theater, plus several
taurants, and exhibition
aces. ✪ *Map H4*

Olympic Green

The Olympic Green will
round the high-tech Olympic
age. It's part of an overall
sterplan to soften the city
th trees, parks, and forested
tways in the run up to 2008.
the heart of the Green is a
gon-shaped lake, the tail of
ich runs by the National
ympic Stadium.

Top 10 Socialist Monuments

1 Agricultural Exhibition Center
In 1959 to celebrate the tenth
anniversary of the People's
Republic of China, this was
one of ten "key" buildings
commissioned in "modern"
Chinese style. ✪ *Map H2*

2 Great Hall of the People
Over 300 rooms large, yet built
in only 10 months. ✪ *Map L5*

3 China National Museum
Every bit as brutal and ugly as
the Great Hall, which it faces
across the square. ✪ *Map M5*

4 Beijing Railway Station
Prime illustration of 1959's
prevailing "size is everything"
approach to architecture.
✪ *Map F4*

5 Cultural Palace of the Nationalities
The one "tenth anniversary"
building of elegance. Its plan
forms the Chinese character
for "mountain." ✪ *Map C4*

6 Minzu Hotel
No Chinese motifs – but
suitably monolithic and drab.
✪ *Map C4*

7 Chinese Military History Museum
Owes a striking debt to
Moscow. ✪ *Map A4*

8 Natural History Museum
Neo-Classical Socialist Chinese
– but nice inside. ✪ *Map E6*

9 National Art Museum of China
The largest art gallery in
China. ✪ *Map M2*

10 Beijing West Railway Station
1995 update on 1959-style
architecture. ✪ *Map A5*

Left **China Railway Museum** Right **Science and Technology Museum**

🔟 Museums

1 **Arthur Sackler Museum**
Part of the Beijing University archeology department, the museum's collection spans 280,000 years, from the Paleolithic era to the Qing dynasty. As well as fossils and bones, it includes beautiful bronzes and fine ceramics.
◎ *Inside Beijing University campus, Haidian district • 6275 1667 • 9am–5pm daily • ¥5*

2 **Ancient Architecture Museum**
Close to the Temple of Heaven, south of Tian'an Men Square, this place is worth visiting for the museum building alone, which is the pavilion of a former grand temple complex (see p74).

3 **Poly Art Museum**
At the Poly Plaza, a shopping mall on the Second Ring Road, consumerism comes with added culture in the form of this small museum of traditional arts and crafts. Exhibits include Buddhas, bodhisattvas, bronzes, and some exquisite bells decorated with animal faces. ◎ *14 Dong Zhi Men N Dajie • Map G2 • 6500 8117 • Subway Dong Si Shi Tiao • 9am–4:30pm Mon–. • ¥50 • www.polymuseum.com*

4 **Imperial City Museum**
After wandering around the Forbidden City, call by this nearby museum to see all the bits of imperial Beijing that did survive. The walls and gates th once encircled the city, along with literally dozens of vanishe temples, are revisited through great many maps, models, and photographs (see p68).

5 **Chinese Military History Museum**
Visitors to the museum are greeted by paintings of Mao, Marx, Lenin, and Stalin, at least two of whom were fully conversant with the various methods of bringing death and destruction celebrated inside. The ground floor is filled with fighter planes, tanks, and missiles, while displays upstair chronicle China's military campaigns (see p91).

Chinese Military History Museum

tural History Museum

China National Museum

What the Met is to New rk and the British Museum London, the China National is Beijing. Unlike the two foreign useums, which are filled with international haul of spoils, is place contains only national easures – and pressive they are o. However, only ommunist Party oupies are likely to preciate the propandist Museum of e Revolution, which kes up the north wing of the ilding (see p67).

China National Museum

Science and Technology Museum

hibits at this suitably hi-tech oking complex start with cient science and come bang -to-date with space capsules d magnetic-levitation ains (see p96).

Natural History Museum

ere are around 000 specimens on splay, including a e collection of odels and skeletons dinosaurs, and other eatures that are en more prehistoric an the Socialist lings of the museum ilding (see p74).

Beijing Police Museum

Housed in the 19th-century former City Bank of New York in the old Legation Quarter, this surprisingly fun museum boasts displays on themes such as the suppression of counter-revolutionaries and drug dealers Famed police dog Feisheng is here – stuffed and mounted – and there are live transmissions from a roadside traffic camera. An interactive screen poses legal questions and correct answers win prizes: it doesn't say what the punishment is for those who answer wrongly. ◎ 36 Dong Jiao Min Xiang • Map M6 • 8522 5018 • Subway: Qian Men • 9am–4pm Tue–Sun • ¥5

China Railway Museum

The recently opened Railway Ministry Science and Technology Center has a vast hall displaying 53 old locomotives, including some of the enormous black engines imported by the Japanese when they controlled Manchuria. The museum is some distance from the center of town, but for steam buffs the 30-minute taxi ride is possibly a small price to pay (see p97).

There are more museums housed in some of the many pavilions of the Forbidden City See pp8–11

43

Left **Incense sticks for sale** Center **South Cathedral** Right **Cow Street Mosque**

Places of Worship

Lama Temple

South Cathedral

Also known as St. Mary's Church, this was Beijing's first Catholic house of worship. It remains the largest functioning church, and has regular services in a variety of languages including Chinese, English, and Latin. Service times are posted on the noticeboard *(see p75)*.

Cow Street Mosque

There are currently about 250,000 Muslims in Beijing. The majority live in the Niu Jie district, which is where you find this mosque, also known as the Niu Jie Mosque. It is the city's oldest and largest Islamic place of worship. Despite being over one thousand years old, the mosque has recently been renovated to the tune of $2.4 million and looks splendid *(see p74)*.

Fayuan Temple

This temple doubles as the city's Buddhist Academy. Founded in 1956, the Academy trains monks to serve in monasteries throughout China. The temple has an excellent collection of effigies, including giant reclining Buddha *(see p75)*

Lama Temple

Formerly one of the most notable centers of Buddhism outside Tibet until it was shut down during the Cultural Revolution. It was reputedly saved from destruction by the intervention of the president, Zhou Enlai. With Buddhism enjoying a resurgence in popularity the precincts are once again home to around 70 monks *(see pp16–17)*.

North Cathedral

Not far west of Bei Hai Park, this cathedral is a twin-towered piece of Gothic confectionery, painted in blue with white trim, like a Wedgwood dish. But the bright façade masks a bloody past: not long after the Jesuits finished the church in 1889 it

Main hall, Fayuan Temple

Previous pages **Detail from Nine-dragon Screen, Bei Hai Park**

me under siege from
Boxers during the
00 rebellion. Many
the congregation
eltering inside were
ed. ◉ *Xishiku Dajie*
ap J2 • Subway: Xidan

Confucius Temple
During the Cultural
volution, Confucianism
s a dirty word and its
mples were converted to other
es, or just abandoned. Recent
ars have seen a U-turn, with
nfucian values being touted
ew by Beijing's leaders, but
s important temple remains
glected *(see p81)*.

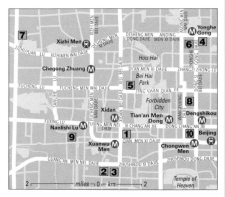

Confucius Temple

Wanshou Temple
Up in the northwest Haidian
trict, the Wanshou (Longevity)
mple is worth a stop en route
the Summer Palace. Looking
unlike a mini Forbidden City,
complex houses the Beijing
Museum – a collection of
torical relics including
nzes, jade, carved lacquer,
d a small but exquisite
ection of Buddha images.
*Kisanhuan Lu, on the north side of
u Qiao Bridge* • *Map A1* • *6845 6997*
bway: Xizhi Men, then taxi • *9am–*
)pm Tue–Sun • *¥20*

St. Joseph's Church
o known as the
st Cathedral, this
n attractive triple-
ned church in the
oque style. It was
t built on the site
he residence of a
uit missionary in
5 and, following
thquakes, fire,
the destruction
ught during the
ker Rebellion, has

had to be rebuilt on a
number of occasions
since. It is fronted by a
gateway and piazza, and
is beautifully lit at night.
◉ *74 Wangfujing Dajie*
• *Map N3* • *6524 0634*
• *Subway: Dengshikou*

White Clouds Temple
Home to the China
Daoist Association, the temple
was founded in AD 739 and is
Beijing's largest Daoist shrine.
Daoism, also known as Taoism,
is a Chinese folk religion, which
centers around maintaining a
positive relationship with several
categories of gods, ghosts, and
ancestral spirits *(see p91)*.

St. Michael's Church
One of the city's less well-
known churches, St. Michael's is
hidden away in the old Legation
Quarter *(see p75)*. It was built in
1901, with three spires in Gothic
style, to serve the area's various
embassies. Narrowly escaping
destruction during the Cultural
Revolution, it was renovated by
the Chinese Patriotic Catholic
Church, to whom it now belongs.
◉ *Dong Jiao Min Xiang* • *Map N5*
• *Subway: Chongwen Men*

Left **Embroidered silk** Center **Carved stone statues** Right **Tea**

🔟 Souvenirs

1 Tea sets

You'll never look at a cup the same way again. For a start, Chinese tea cups are often three-piece affairs with a saucer to prevent burned fingers and a lid to keep the leaves out of your mouth. They are sized from mug to thimble, and the colors and patterning can be exquisite, making a nicely-boxed tea set the number one gift from China.

2 Tea

All over Beijing are shops devoted to tea. One street specializes in nothing else with dozens of shops together offering around 500 different varieties of leaf. The packaging can often be quite beautiful too, from bright red tins to cardboard-tube containers decorated with a waving Mao.

3 Contemporary art

Not just a striking souvenir but also a potential investment. Collecting Chinese art is big

Painted scroll

business and some name go for tens of thousands dollars at international auction. However, there's lot of fine work exhibited galleries all over Beijing that is far more affordab

4 Silk

A Chinese invention and still widely employe today for fine-quality clothing and embroidery. Genuine silk garments a expensive but look out for cheaper household accessories such as s cushions or bags.

5 Calligraphy

It's a skill that is as revere as painting. Master calligraphe practice their art assiduously, and their works can be very expensive. However, hanging wall scrolls are available at affordable prices and make beautiful souvenirs, especially for anyone with an appropriate Zen-like apartment back home

6 Marble chops

A chop is a signature, carv onto wood, marble, stone or, these days, plastic, and used a a stamp on official documents or contracts. It is impossible t do business in China without a chop. You can quickly and easi get your own by having your name translated into Chinese characters and taking it along to a chop-maker.

Chinese tea set

Mao memorabilia
The great icon, Mao appears posters, badges, banners, and most anything else with a flat face. There are shops and lls that trade in nothing but o in the Dazhalan district and Panjiayuan Market.

Ceramics
China has been oducing ceramics centuries. The est come from gdezhen, and can seen at Ceramic y at 277 Wangfujing jie. Just remember, you have get it home in one piece.

Lanterns and lamps
The beautiful red lanterns t see you see hanging all over jing make a fantastic and very ordable souvenir of China. An ually attractive variant are the le lamps with distinctive red, p-shaped shades. These should st no more than a few yuan.

Designer clothing
Hottest souvenirs from jing are top-label international nds, sold here for a fraction the cost back home. They are of course, fakes – almost ssable copies but poorer ality. Those whose copyrights being infringed have begun take legal action and the days the fakes may be numbered.

memorabilia

Top 10 Galleries

1 798 Space
For contemporary art the place to go is the 798 Art District, and this is the gallery that started it all *(see p24)*.

2 CourtYard Gallery
Basement gallery attached to classy restaurant *(see p60)*. www.courtyard-gallery.com

3 Red Gate Gallery
Art in a 15th-century city watchtower *(see p85)*. www.redgategallery.com

4 Beijing Arts & Crafts Central Store
Possibly the best souvenir store in town, filled with silks ceramics, jade, calligraphy, and paintings *(see p70)*.

5 Imperial Archive
An impressive complex to wander around and art for sale in some of the halls. ◈ *136 Nan Chizi Dajie • Map M4*

6 China Art Seasons
A high-ceilinged space well suited to large-scale sculpture *(see p25)*. www.artseasons.com.sg

7 Beijing Art Now
Exciting art space in the grounds of the Workers' Stadium. www.artnow.cn

8 Green T. House
Art here has to compete with Beijing's wackiest bit of interior design *(see p60)*. www.greenteahouse.com.cn

9 Timezone 8
Art book store with a small gallery specializing in photography *(see p25)*. www.timezone8.com

10 Zen Cat Gallery
Unique gallery on the shores of Hou Hai (14 Hou Hai Nanyan) that acts as a show space for the eye-catching creations of kooky artist Dong Zi. ◈ *Map D2*

For Beijing's Top 10 markets and malls See pp50–51

Left **Hong Qiao Market** Right **Panjiayuan Antique Market**

Markets and Malls

Oriental Plaza

1 Hong Qiao Market
Best known for pearls (hence its alternative name, the "Pearl Market"), with a huge range available, freshwater and seawater, up on the third floor. The floors below are a tight compress of clothing, shoes, electronics, and more, while in the basement is a pungent, but fascinating market for fish, frogs, and snakes (see p76).

2 Oriental Plaza
A large mall that stretches a whole city block and boasts several levels of top-end retailers including Paul Smith, Swarovski, Sisley, Max Mara, and Apple. There are also a couple of supermarkets, a sizeable pharmacy, a big CD and DVD store, and an excellent food court (see also p70).

3 Silk Market
More properly known as Xiushui, this is the most infamous market in Beijing. It is reportedly the city's third main tourist attraction after the Forbidden City and the Great Wall. Some 100,000 shoppers a day visit to snap up famous brand goods for ridiculously low prices. Of course, they are all fakes, but who's to know? However, visitors may not have to struggle with the morality of all for much longer, as the trade in counterfeits is likely to be stamped out before the Olympic come to town (see also p88).

4 Yaxiu Market
At the center of the embassy district of Sanlitun, Yaxiu (or Yashow) offers more of the same as the Silk Market four floors of clothing, bags, shoes, and sportswear, plus some jewelry, nail salons, and bunch of tailors on the top floor who can run up a gent's suit for around ¥350 (see also p88).

5 Panjiayuan Antique Market
As much a tourist attraction as shopping experience, Panjiayuan

Beijing shopper

is home to around 3,0 dealers peddling everything from broke bicycles to family heirlooms. Come for Mao memorabilia, a Qing-dynasty vase, or yellowing Tintin comic in Chinese. The marke kicks off daily at 4:30a and is at its busiest, best, and most chaoti at the weekends.

erious collectors swoop at
awn, but it's fun any time.
*Panjiayuan Qiao • Map H6 • 6775 2405
• Subway: Guomao, then taxi • Open
30am–2:30pm daily*

China World Shopping Mall

eijing's ritziest mall is attached
 the equally luxurious China
Vorld Hotel. The mall, which
 also known as Guomao,
 home to elite international
'ands such as Moschino, Prada,
artier, and Louis Vuitton. Prices
e at least as expensive as
ack home *(see also p88)*.

Dong Jiao Wholesale Market

a series of hangar-like
uildings southeast of SOHO,
aders sell just about anything
id everything. It is where
staurants and hotels buy pots
id pans, schools come for
assroom supplies, service
aff buy uniforms, and
nall traders and
oks come for fresh
uit and vegetables.
u may not need a
rton of 1,000 chopsticks,
t it is fascinating to
owse, all the same.
*Dong Si Huan Zhong Lu, west of Sihui
idge • Map G4 • Subway: Guomao*

Lai Tai Market

This covered market, just
rth of the Third Ring Road,
t far from the Kempinski hotel,
an appealing mix of garden
nter and tropical fish store.
alf the vast ground floor is
ed with bamboo, cactus, and
namental rockeries, while the
her half is all large aquariums
brightly colored marine life –
us ceramics downstairs.
*Nuren Jie, off Xiaoyun Lu • Map H1
Subway: Dong Zhi Men, then taxi*

Bead stall at Yaxiu Market

Aliens Street Market

Bizarre name, but the aliens
in question are the Russians,
who do most of the buying and
selling here *(see also p88)*.

Grand World Electrical Market

Pick up a used mobile phone for
under ¥300, or a new model for
two-thirds the normal retail price.
Aside from phones, there are
three floors packed with
TVs, CD and mp3 players,
and games consoles.
*Nuren Jie, off Xiaoyun Lu
• Map H1 • Subway: Dong Zhi
Men, then taxi*

Beaded purse

Beijing's Top 10

Left **Natural History Museum** Center **China Ethnic Culture Park** Right **At play in the park**

Children's Attractions

Beijing Amusement Park
An old-style fairground with a Ferris wheel, teacup merry-go-round, mini rollercoaster, and go-kart track set lakeside in grassy Long Tan Park. Avoid at weekends and on public holidays, when the place gets uncomfortably crowded. ◉ *1 Zuo'an Men Nei Dajie, west entrance Long Tan Park • Map F6 • 6711 1155 • Subway: Tiantan Dong Men • Jul, Aug 9am–8:30pm daily. Sep–Mar 9am–6pm daily • ¥100; children ¥70; under 4 ft (1.1 m) free*

Beijing Zoo
Most children will remain happily oblivious to the poor conditions that many of the animals are kept in and which are likely to upset older animal lovers. However, the pandas are well cared for and the setting is pleasant and leafy *(see p92)*.

Beijing Aquarium
Located in the northeastern corner of the zoo, this is a new and very impressive attraction,

Pandas at Beijing Zoo

which will keep children happy for hours, especially the dolphin shows *(see p92)*.

Fundazzle
Fundazzle is a massive indoor kid's playground. Loud and bright, it has a two-story jungle gym, a vast plastic ball-filled pool, trampolines, swings, and a host of other activities and enticements with which to reward young children who've just had to endure hours of being dragged round the Forbidden City. ◉ *Gongren Tiyuchang Nan Lu, south side of Workers' Stadium • Map G • 6500 4193 • Subway: Chaoyang Men 9am–5:pm Mon–Fri; 9am–7pm Sat, Sun ¥30 for 2 hrs • www.fandoule.com*

Natural History Museum
As long as you steer them clear of the horror show that is the exhibit of partially dissected human bodies, children will love the giant animatronic dinosaurs and prehistoric skeletons, as well as the plethora of stuffed animals of all species and sizes *(see p74)*.

China Ethnic Culture Park
Like an overgrown model village, "China World" is filled with colorful models of buildings representing all the nation's many and varied ethnic minorities. Some of the models are huge, and it's all very colorful, as are the regular performances by ethnic musicians and singers in full costume *(see p96)*.

eijing Aquarium at Beijing Zoo

Blue Zoo Beijing

Not to be confused with eijing Zoo, this is a small but eautifully done aquarium. It has n enormous coral reef tank ontaining an array of visually xciting marine life, including els, rays, and sharks. A big us is that the tanks are set low hough that toddlers can peer to them. There's also a "marine nnel" and twice-daily shark eding sessions (see p86).

Science and Technology Museum

ots of hands-on and interactive xhibits for children to pull, push, d even walk through. There is so an Imax-style movie theater d an indoor play area on the ird and fourth floors a separate building orth of the main ntrance (see p96).

Happy Valley

Disneyland-style eme park divided to six themed gions, with 120 tractions. The park's m is to keep both rents and children ntent by providing teractive education xperiences. Thrill-eekers can enjoy no ss than 40 rides, of

which ten are "extreme," including a "Drop Tower" in which riders fall at 45 mph (72 km/h) in a terrifying simulated plunge to earth. There is also a shopping complex, and an IMAX cinema.
⊗ Sifang, just off the Fourth Ring Road • 6738 3333 • 9:30am–8pm daily • ¥120; ¥60 children; under 4 ft (1.2 m) free

New China Children's Store

A monster children's store on Beijing's main shopping street, with four floors of everything from carry cots and strollers to masses of local and imported toys. There's even an in-store play area. ⊗ 168 Wangfujing Dajie • Map N4 • 6528 1774 • Subway: Wangfujing • 9am–9:30pm daily

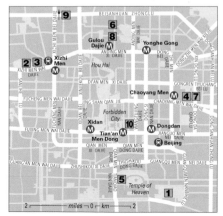

Most Chinese restaurants tend to be children friendly. The Bookworm in Sanlitun has a children's reading corner. See p61

53

Left **Rock at the Workers' Gymnasium** Right **Football at the Workers' Stadium**

Entertainment

Acrobatics
China has a worldwide reputation for its gymnasts, who perform breathtaking routines that showcase their unnerving flexibility. Displays of balance often involve props such as chairs, plates, and bicycles. Several Beijing theaters put on shows, of which the best is possibly that at the Chaoyang Theater (Dong Sanhuan Bei Lu; map H3); your hotel will be able to help with reservations.

Beijing Opera performer

Beijing Opera
With its incomprehensible plots, unfamiliar sounds, and performances lasting up to three hours, Beijing Opera is a hard-to-acquire taste. However, everyone should try it at least once *(see pp38–9)*.

Cinema
The low cost and widespread availability of pirate DVDs means that most Beijingers stay home to watch their movies. So despite a vibrant home movie industry, decent cinemas are few in number. Add to which, there is a cap on the number of imported foreign-language films shown each year.

Classical music
Take the chance to attend a Chinese orchestra performance if at all possible. Sections of unfamiliar plucked string, bowed string, woodwind and percussion instruments compete for attention in swirling arrangements. The main venues are the Forbidden City Concert Hall in Zhong Shan Park and the National Grand Theater *(see p67)*.

Martial arts
The Shaolin monks from Songshan in Henan Province have gained an international reputation for their martial arts prowess. They perform regularly at the Li Yun Theater *(see p39)*.

Puppet theater
Shadow-puppet theater is an art form that has been performed more or less unchanged in China since the 3rd century AD. Shows employ many of the story lines and musical styles of Beijing

Acrobatic show

era, while the puppets can
e quite elaborate and colorfully
essed. The best place to catch
performance is at the China
uppet Art Theater (Anhua Xili,
f Bei Sanhuan Lu).

Rock and pop
Beijing is the Chinese city
ith all the best tunes. It has a
riving music scene supported
a host of small music bars
d clubs (see p63). Punk and
etal thrive but of far more
terest are local folk rockers
no mix ethnic instrumentation
th Western genres.

Sports
Football's big in Beijing. The
cal boys are Beijing Hyundai
uo'an, who play at the Workers'
adium (see p86). Getting
kets is rarely a problem: you
n just show up at the stadium
game day. Second in
pularity is basketball. Top team
e Aoshen who play at the
ijing Guang'an Gymnasium
aiguang Lu; map C6).

Teahouses
You shouldn't leave Beijing
thout visiting a teahouse. Tea
served with great ceremony,
mplete with smellings and
citations of Confucian sayings
d poetry. The price of the tea
ries greatly according to
ality. For venues, see p59.

Theater
Beijing is home to several
cellent theaters, where a few
tablished troupes perform
gularly. Canonical works such
Lao She's "Teahouse" are
creasingly supplemented by
g-budget Western musicals
ch as "Rent" and "Aladdin on
e". See the English-language
ess for what's on.

Top 10 Chinese Movies

1 Beijing Bicycle
(Wang Xiaoshuai; 2001)
A young bike messenger has
his ride stolen and attempts
to get it back.

2 Spring in a Small Town
(Fei Mu; 1948) A man returns
home to find his childhood
sweetheart married. Voted
best Chinese film of all time.

3 Yellow Earth
(Chen Kaige; 1984) A Red
Army soldier is posted to a
desolate province to collect
folk songs and finds misery.

4 Platform
(Jia Zhangke; 2000) Epic
account of the changes in
China's pop culture during
the 1980s.

5 To Live
(Zhang Yimou; 1994)
Tragedy and black humor in
the tale of one family from
the 1940s to the 1980s.

6 A Touch of Zen
(King Hu; 1969), Sword-
play films, have been popular
in China since the 1920s, but
this revitalized the genre.

7 Raise the Red Lantern
(Zhang Yimou; 1991)
Intrigue between the multiple
wives of a wealthy overlord.

8 Farewell My Concubine
(Chen Kaige; 1993) The film
that really put Chinese cinema
back on the map.

9 Hero
(Zhang Yimou; 2002)
Martial arts waltz that to date
is the most successful film
ever made in China.

10 Peacock
(Gu Changwei; 2005) The
tribulations of a working-class
family in a small rural town.

Left **Tea being poured in a Beijing restaurant** Center **Lamb and scallions** Right **Dumplings**

Beijing Dishes

Beijing duck

Beijing duck

1 Beijing duck
The best-known dish in north Chinese cuisine. The duck, a local Beijing variety, is dried and brushed with a sweet marinade before being roasted over fragrant wood chips. It is carved by the chef and eaten wrapped in pancakes with slivered scallions (spring onions) and cucumber.

2 Hotpot
Introduced to Beijing in the 13th century by the invading Mongols, hotpot is a much-loved staple. Literally hundreds of restaurants across the city sell nothing else but. It's a great group dish, with everybody sat around a large bubbling pot of broth dropping in their own shavings of meat, noodles, and vegetables to cook.

3 Zha jiang mian
The name means "clanging dish noodles" – like hot pot, ingredients are added at the table to a central tureen of noodles, and the bowls are loudly clanged together as each dish goes in, hence the name.

4 Jiaozi
The traditional Beijing dumplings are filled with po bai cai (Chinese leaf), and ginger but, in fact, fillings are endless. You can find jiaozi at snack shops all ove the city. They are also sold on the street, served from a giant hot plate over a brazier.

5 Thousand-year-old eggs
These are raw duck eggs that have been put into mud, chalk and ammonia and left, no for a thousand years, but more like two weeks. When retrieved the egg is steamed or hard-boiled: the white has turned a greenish-black. The eggs are cu up and sprinkled with soy sauc and sesame oil.

6 Lao mian
Watching a cook make lao mian (hand-pulled noodles) is almost as enjoyable as eating

Hotpot

Beijing's Top 10

For Beijing's best Chinese restaurants See pp58–9

weet and sour carp

em. First the dough is
tretched and then swung
e a skipping rope, so that it
ecomes plaited. The process
repeated until the strands
f dough are as thin as string.

Lamb and scallions
Scallions (spring onions) are
common Beijing ingredient and
this dish they are rapidly stir-
ied along with sliced lamb,
arlic, and a sweet-bean paste.

Sweet and sour carp
Beijing cooking is heavily
fluenced by the cuisine of
handong Province, generally
garded as the oldest and best
China. Sweet and sour carp is
quintessential Shandong dish
aditionally made with fish from
e Yellow River.

Drunken empress chicken
Supposedly named after
ang Guifei, an imperial concubine
verly fond of her alcohol. The
sh is prepared using Chinese
ine and is served cold.

Stir-fried kidney flowers
These are actually pork
dneys cut in a criss-cross fashion
d stir-fried, during which they
en out like "flowers". The
dneys are typically prepared
ith bamboo shoots, water
estnuts, and edible black
ngus (a sort of mushroom).

Top 10 Beijing Street Foods

1 Lu da gun'r
Literally "donkeys rolling in dirt": sweet red-bean paste in a rice dough dusted with peanut powder.

2 Jian bing
Chinese crêpe. Often sold off the back of tricycles and a typical Beijing breakfast.

3 Shao bing
Hot bread roll filled with a fried egg and often sprinkled with aniseed for flavoring.

4 Tang chao lizi
Chestnuts, roasted in hot sand and served in a paper bag. A seasonal snack appearing in autumn.

5 Tang hu lu
A kabob of candied hawthorn berries.

6 Chuan'r
In any area with lots of bars and clubs you'll find street vendors selling *chuan'r* (kabobs). They cost just a few *yuan* per skewer.

7 Can yong
Like a kabob but this version involves silk worms. The grubs are first boiled and skewered, and then grilled to order. They are supposedly high in protein.

8 Rou bing
Cooked bread filled with finely chopped and spiced pork. A variant is *rou jiamo*, which is a bun filled with diced lamb.

9 You tiao
Deep-fried dough sticks, often dipped in warm congee (a rice porridge).

10 Hong shu
A winter specialty, these are baked sweet potatoes, often heated in ovens made from oil drums.

Left **Bellagio** Right **Beijing Dadong Roast Duck Restaurant**

🔟 Chinese Restaurants

Foil-baked fish dish, Han Cang

1 Beijing Dadong Roast Duck Restaurant
Lots of restaurants specialize in Beijing's most famous dish, and debate rages endlessly over who serves the best fowl. This place is less over-blown and over-priced than many of its rivals, and for that it gets our vote *(see p89)*.

2 Guizhou Luo Luo Suan Tang Yu
Sharing a hotpot is an essential Beijing experience and there's no better place to do it than on beguiling "Ghost Street." The décor may be a bit dingy but ingredients are fresh and the broth and dipping sauces are terrific *(see p89)*.

3 Three Guizhou Men
Authentic Guizhou food, uncompromisingly spicy and sour, is generally too coarse for foreign tastes, but here it is blended with more conventional Chinese flavors. The atmosphere

is stylish, in keeping with the local hipster fondness for minority cuisines *(see p89)*.

4 Han Cang
Little known even in China, the cuisine of the southeastern Hakka people is a delight. They use heaps of hot salt to bake chicken and fish, and do lots of dishes featuring smoky pork. Han Cang does excellent Hakka dishes and has a fun and vibran atmosphere to boot *(see p83)*.

5 Bellagio
A supremely hip and stylish Taiwanese chain, also serving quality Hakka dishes. Everything looks stunning and it tastes eve better. Leave room for one of th hugely popular red-bean ice desserts *(see p89)*.

6 Made In China
The kitchen is open allowin diners to view ducks roasting and nimble fingers speedily making disks of dough and spooning in fragrant fillings to make the little dumplings know as *jiaozi*, a Beijing specialty *(see p56)*.

Made In China

7 Princess Mansion
Qing court kitsch doesn't get much more over the top than this: wait staff dolled up in traditional dress, while dances and songs are performed throughout dinner. Touristy? Yes, bu

paring Beijing duck

e Qing court-styled food is
cellent and you are ensured a
emorable evening *(see p71)*.

Afunti
The most famous and
pular Uighur establishment in
ijing, specializing in Muslim
njiang cuisine. Expect lots of
nb, skewered and roasted, in
dition to after-dinner table-top
ncing and live music *(see p89)*.

Huang Ting
A beautiful restaurant:
ecreation of a traditional
eyuan (courtyard) house
using thousands of bricks from
molished properties, along
th wooden screens, carved
one friezes, and door guardian
ones. Dishes lean towards the
ntonese, but there are also
ijing favorites, including classic
ijing roast duck *(see p56)*.

South Silk Road
A fashionable, superior chain
vned by a Beijing-based artist
rving authentic Yunnanese
od. Diners can sample all
anner of flowers, insects,
d mysterious animal parts,
well as more conventional
shes *(see p83)*.

Top 10 Teahouses

1 China Huangzhou Westlake Tearoom
Lively, with music at the
weekends. ✆ *Sanlihe Dong
Lu • Map B4*

2 Confucius Teahouse
Just across from the
Confucius Temple. English
spoken. ✆ *28 Guozijian Lu
• Map F1*

3 Da Hong Pao Teahouse
Stone-top tables and tree-
stump seats, but a bit out of
the way up in Haidian. ✆ *Fuwu
Lu, off Cuiwei Nan Li*

4 Hong Hao Ge
Bamboo décor beside
a park behind the Military
History Museum. ✆ *9 Yuyuan
Tan Nan Lu • Map A4*

5 Lao She Teahouse
Tea plus acrobatics, magic
tricks, and Beijing Opera. ✆ *3
Qian Men Xi Dajie • Map K6*

6 Ming Ren Teahouse
A chain of teahouses; this
branch is conveniently close
to Hou Hai. ✆ *Building 3,
Ping'an Dajie • Map K1*

7 Purple Vine
Lovely place located just
outside the west gate of the
Forbidden City. ✆ *2 Nan Chang
Jie • Map L4*

8 Xi Hua Yuan Teahouse
Decorated with ornate
Qing-style furniture. Just over
the road from the Purple Vine.
✆ *Bei Chang Jie • Map L4*

9 Ji Gu Ge Teahouse
Popular teahouse in area
of antique shops south of
Tian'an Men Square. ✆ *132–6
Liulichang Dongjie • Map D5*

10 Tian Qiao Happy Teahouse
Tea ceremonies with food and
bite-sized cultural morsels at
the upstairs theater. ✆ *1 Bei
Wei Lu • Map E6*

*For more on the different Chinese dishes found in Beijing's
restaurants* See pp56–7

Left **Green T. House** Right **Cafe Sambal**

TOP10 International Restaurants

Alameda

1 Alameda
The look is LA or Sydney, the food is Brazilian. The well balanced menu includes good-value set lunches and dinners that change with the availability of fresh ingredients but great steaks are standard *(see p89)*.

2 Cafe Sambal
Sambal, a sauce made with chillies, features on the menu at this stylish Malay restaurant, along with other Southeast Asian specialties. The food is complemented by a beautiful courtyard-house setting *(see p82)*.

3 Hatsune
Hatsune has a dedicated following for its beautiful sushi rolls, prepared with fresh fish flown from Japan. It also looks gorgeous and has superlative service. On top of which, it is also a lot cheaper than you might imagine *(see p89)*.

4 Aria
Contemporary Western cuisine that combines top-qual ingredients with impressive cooking skills. A multi-course option with wine pairings provides a tour of an inventive but never pretentious Asian-French fusion menu that's pure pleasure *(see p89)*.

5 CourtYard
The location (facing the ea gate of the Forbidden City) vie with the food (international fusion) for top honors. For the best views ask for a window table; if they are taken, instead enjoy the striking contemporar art on the walls *(see p71)*.

6 Green T. House
With its vast empty spaces and furniture so over-designed that the chairs and tables are scarcely recognizable as such, Green T. House seems more gallery than restaurant. The strangeness extends to the menu: from roast lamb with oolong and fennel, to green tea wasabi prawns, everything contains tea *(see p89)*.

Hatsune

rtYard

Nuage
The setting is a two-story
ooden mansion on the banks
Qian Hai, overlooking the lake.
e Vietnamese food is variable
t as a romantic night-time
ing spot this takes some
ating (see p82).

Jing
A beautiful modernist
staurant dominated by a vast
eaming open kitchen. Watching
eam of white-hatted chefs
aring, caramelizing, and flash-
ing is a sure way to build up
appetite, and the wine list is
emplary (see p71).

RBL
An ultra-stylish diner offering
ntemporary fusion food built
ound a sushi bar. Attached bar,
house, doubles as a blues
b, and is intriguing for its
tting in a former imperial cold
orage room (see p71).

Morel's
One of the oldest Western
staurants in town is this
mely spot serving simple,
gh quality Belgian fare. As an
companiment to the food, the
t of Belgian beers is second to
ne (see p89).

Top 10 Places to Snack

1 The Tree
Popular Sanlitun pub that
does excellent wood-fired
pizzas (see p63).

2 Fish Nation
Fish and chips English
style in an old *hutong* setting
(see p83).

3 Schlotzky's
US-style deli for pastrami
on rye and all the rest of it.
⊗ Pacific Century Place, Gongren
Tiyuchang Bei Lu • Map H2

4 The Bookworm
Lending library, bar, and
a great place for healthy light
lunches. ⊗ Building 4, Sanlitun
Nan Lu • Map H2

5 Oriental Plaza Food Court
A huge array of international
fast foods at the bottom of
Wangfujing (see p71).

6 Kiosk
Excellent meaty subs and
sandwiches in an open-air
setting. ⊗ Na Li Mall, off
Sanlitun Bei Lu • Map H2

7 AT Café
Quirky café in the the 798
Art District with a limited but
appealing menu (see p24).

8 Du Yichu
Age-old restaurant that
specializes in *baozi* (steamed
buns). ⊗ 36 Qian Men Dajie,
corner of Dazhalan Jie • Map E5

9 Wangfujing Snack Street
Kabob, noodle, and soup
stalls fill a narrow alley off the
bottom end of Wangfujing
Dajie. ⊗ Map M4

10 Coolgel
Excellent gelateria, and
cheap too at ¥5 per scoop.
⊗ Tian'an Men Square, east side
• Map L5

Left **No Name Bar** Center **Souk** Right **Centro**

🔟 Bars and Pubs

1 Bed Tapas & Bar
The perfect Beijing bar – an old courtyard house kitted out with antique furniture, including *kang*-style beds. Excellent food, plus weekend DJs *(see p82)*.

2 Centro
Beijing's classiest bar is off the lobby of one of the city's swankiest hotels. Louche and loungey, it boasts live jazz, sexy waitresses, and the last word in cocktails. ✪ *Kerry Center Hotel, 1 Guanghua Lu • Map H4 • 6561 8833 ext. 6296 • Subway: Guomao*

3 Drum & Bell
A terrific location between the Drum and Bell Towers, and an appealing mix of aged furniture, Cultural Revolution memorabilia, cheap Tsingtao beer, and friendly staff *(see p82)*.

4 No Name Bar
The oldest Hou Hai bar is also the best, with a ramshackle charm that defeats the copyists. Heated by wood-burning stoves, or cooled by lake breezes, it's perfect year-round *(see p82)*.

Drum & Bell

Bed Tapas & Bar

5 Pass By Bar
On a *hutong* dotted with several hostels, Pass By is a we established travelers' haunt. Tw attractive rooms wrap around a pretty courtyard; food is a cut above, and there's a lending library and guidebooks for sale *(see p82)*.

6 Red Moon
Where Beijing's smart set mingles with Executive Class visitors. This is the sleek house bar of one of the city's most high-powered hotels. Dress to impress for cocktails, sushi bar and cigar lounge. Quality, of course, comes at a price. ✪ *Gra Hyatt, 1 Dong Chang'an Jie• Map N5 • 8518 1234 • Subway: Wangfujing*

7 Souk
Tucked behind Annie's restaurant near the west gate Chaoyang Park, Souk is where

e Middle East (in the form of
ookahs and Lebanese cuisine)
eets the Far East. There are
e obligatory *kang*-style beds
r lounging and a courtyard for
fresco drinking, as well as
eekend DJs. ✪ *West gate of
aoyang Park • 6506 7309*

Stone Boat
While it may not be as
storically significant as its
amesake up at the Summer
lace, this Stone Boat does a
od latte, it's a WiFi hotspot
d, come evening, it serves as
unique, candlelit venue for a
iet drink. ✪ *Ri Tan Park • Map G4
6501 9986 • Subway: Yongan Li*

The Tree
A huge favorite among the
ty's expats, this is a convivial,
one-floored pub that marries
fantastic array of beers (40
elgian brews alone) with
ccellent wood-fired pizzas.
43 Sanlitun Bei Jie • Map H2 • 6415
54 • Subway: Dong Si Shi Tiao

World of Suzie Wong
The name is from a novel
out a prostitute, but this Suzie
ong is wholly respectable. It
t the mark for the "opium den-
yle" popular in Beijing bar-land
d it's stayed ahead of the pack
anks to its guaranteed good-
ne for all. ✪ *West gate of Chaoyang
rk • 6593 6049*

rld of Suzie Wong

Top 10 Music Bars

1 2 Kolegas Bar
Live music bar at a drive-in
movie theater. Two miles east
of the Lufthansa Center. ✪ *21
Liang Ma Qiao Lu • 8196 4820*

2 13 Club
Hardcore venue in the
university district of Haidian.
✪ *161 Lanqiying • 8262 8077*

3 Browns
Live jazz every Thursday
from 9pm. ✪ *4 Gongren
Tiyuchang Bei Lu • Map H3
• 6591 2717*

4 CD Jazz Café
Beijing's only dedicated
jazz venue. ✪ *16 Dongsanhuan
Bei Lu • Map H2 • 6506 8288*

5 Icehouse
Blues bar attached to RBL
(see p71). ✪ *53 Dong'an Men
Dajie • Map M4 • 6522 1389*

6 Nameless Highland
Expect anything from
Mongolian folk to Japanese
punk and Chinese Britpop.
✪ *Building 14, Area 1, Anhuili,
Yayuncun • 6489 1613*

7 New Get Lucky
Nuren Jie bar majoring in
Chinese rock, roots, and folk.
✪ *Xingba Lu • Map H1 • 8448
3335*

8 The Tree
The music is incidental to
the business of drinking, but
the occasional act impresses
(see left).

9 What? Bar
Terrific little, indie-oriented
music bar close by the west
gate of the Forbidden City.
✪ *72 Bei Chang Jie • Map L3
• 139 1020 9249*

10 Yugong Yishan
The city's most satisfying
music venue, with an eclectic
but always laudable booking
policy. ✪ *1 Gongren Tiyuchang
Bei Lu • Map G2 • 6415 0687*

Beijing's bars are normally open from around noon until 2am

AROUND
TOWN

BEIJING'S TOP 10

Tian'an Men Square

Tian'an Men Square and the Forbidden City

THE GEOGRAPHICAL, SPIRITUAL, AND HISTORICAL *heart of Beijing, Tian'*
Men Square and the Forbidden City together represent a yin and yang
arrangement; one is a mind-bogglingly vast, empty, rectangular public spa
the other is an even more massive, rectangular walled private enclosure. O
represents modern China, complete with its Socialist monuments, refrigerat
Great Leader and resonances of recent political upheaval, while the other i
a silent repository of ancient imperial glories. There is enough to see aroun
the square and in the Forbidden City to make it worth setting aside a whol
day for each. One day will present a vivid
impression of China as it was, and the other an
equally striking portrait of the country as it is now.
And after all that, wander around the corner for
a look at the new National Grand Theater and a
glimpse of the China of the future.

Mao's Mausoleum

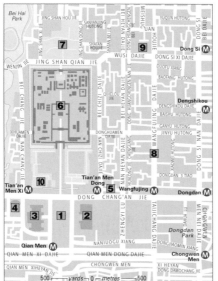

🔟 Sights

1. Tian'an Men Square
2. China National Museum
3. Great Hall of the People
4. National Grand Theater
5. Imperial City Museum
6. Forbidden City
7. Jing Shan Park
8. Wangfujing Street
9. National Art Museum of China
10. Zhongshan Park

Previous pages **Tiled gateway at the Forbidden City**

Tian'an Men Square

Although now thoroughly synonymous with Beijing, until relatively recently there was no Tian'an Men Square. For centuries this was just a main thoroughfare leading to the Gate of Heavenly Peace (Tian'an Men) and the approach to the Forbidden City. The area was cleared in the first half of the 20th century, then quadrupled in size in 1959, supposedly allowing for up to one million people to gather. Many of the buildings flanking the square were erected at this time (see pp14–15).

China National Museum

Two museums in one, this imposing building houses both the Museum of Chinese History and the Museum of the Revolution. Of the two, the former is by far the more interesting, with an unsurpassed collection of great works of Chinese art; the halls are also used for temporary exhibitions. The rather dull Museum of the Revolution contains models, documents, and photographs connected with the history of the Chinese Communist Party – for political enthusiasts only. ◈ East side of Tian'an Men Square • Map M5 • 6512 [...]01 • Subway: Tian'an Men Dong • Jul, [...] 8am–6pm daily. Sep–Jun 9am–4pm. [La]st admission 1 hr before closing. • ¥30

Great Hall of the People

Great Hall of the People

This the Chinese parliament building, home of the nation's legislative body, the National People's Congress. Regular tours visit the banquet room where US President Nixon dined in 1972 and the 10,000-seat auditorium with its ceiling inset with a massive red star. The building is closed to the public when the Congress is in session. ◈ West side of Tian'an Men Square • Map L5 • 6605 6847 • Subway: Tian'an Men Xi • 9am–3pm daily • ¥30

Tian'an Men traffic policeman

National Grand Theater

Completed in 2006, Beijing's new opera house is already a major city landmark. Designed by French architect Paul Andreu, it is built of glass and titanium and takes the form of a giant parabolic dome – earning it the nickname the "Giant Egg." The high-tech lighting that illuminates the exterior is reflected in a moat, while the entrance is through an underwater tunnel. ◈ Map K5 • Subway: Tian'an Men Xi

National Grand Theater

For more modern architecture **See pp40–41**

Around Town – Tian'an Men Square and the Forbidden City

The cult of Mao

Mao was an ideologue whose impatience at the pace of reform often brought disaster. Skilful maneuvering by the Party meant that he remained a heroic figure. The years after his death saw a diminishing of his status, but since the 1990s his popularity has revived. Once again he is considered by millions to be *weida* – Great.

Imperial City Museum

Much of the Imperial City of Beijing was destroyed under the Communists. A model in the museum illustrates the extent of what has been lost, including the wall that once encircled the city, the gates, and a great many temples. There are also exhibits on the *hutongs*, plus collections of armor, weapons, and ceramics. ✆ 9 Changpu Heyan • Map M5 • 8511 5104 • Subway: Tian'an Men Dong • 9am–5:30pm daily • ¥20 • Audio tour ¥50

Wangfujing street sculptures

Forbidden City

The Forbidden City is Beijing's top "must-see" sight. A seemingly endless collection of pavilions, gates, courts, and gardens, the complex encompasses five

centuries of colorful, occasional lurid, imperial history. Trying to see everything in one go will bring on a severe case of Ming fatigue and it is recommended that you tackle the palace over at least two visits *(see pp8–11)*

Jing Shan Park

Jing Shan (Prospect Hill) lies immediately north of the Forbidden City. The hill was created from the earth that was excavated while building the moat around the palace comple during the reign of the Ming Yongle emperor. The hill's purpose was to protect the emperor and his court from malign northern influences which brought death and destruction according to classical *feng shui*. The park is dotted with pavilions and halls, but the highlight is the superb view south from the hill-top Wancheng Pavilion. ✆ 1 Wenjin Jie • Map L2 • 6404 4071 • Subway Tian'an Men Xi • 7am 8pm daily • ¥2

Wangfujing Dajie

Beijing's main shopping street is filled with department stores and giant malls *(see p7C* as well as stores selling silk, te and shoes. However, the

Left **Forbidden City** Right **Wangfujing Dajie shopping street**

National Art Museum of China

ghlight is the Night Market
ith its range of open-air food
talls *(see p71)*. A little to the
orth is St. Joseph's, one of the
ty's most important churches,
ecently restored at a cost of
S$2 million *(see p47)*. ◎ Map N4
Subway: Wangfujing • Night Market:
30pm–10pm daily

National Art Museum of China

he largest art gallery in China
vas one of ten key buildings
rected in 1959 to celebrate the
enth anniversary of the founding
f the People's Republic. It has
o permanent collection, rather
s 14 halls, which are spread
ver three floors, are employed
o host a constant rotation of
emporary exhibitions of Chinese
nd international art. ◎ *1 Wusi
ajie • Map M2 • 6401 6234 • Subway:
ong Si • 9am–5pm daily, last entry 4pm
¥20*

Zhong Shan Park

Northwest of the Tian'an
len, Zong Shan (also known as
un Yat Sen Park) offers respite
om the crowds thronging the
earby sights. The park was once
art of the grounds of a temple
nd the square Altar of Earth and
arvests remains. In the eastern
ection is the Forbidden City
oncert Hall, Beijing's premier
enue for classical music. ◎ *Map
4 • 6605 2528 • Subway: Tian'an Men Xi
6am–10pm daily • ¥3*

A Day Around Tian'an Men Square and Wangfujing Dajie

Morning

🕐 Arrive early to beat
the crowds at **Mao's
Mausoleum** *(see p14)*
and shuffle through for the
permitted few minutes in
the presence of the Great
Helmsman. The Forbidden
City can be saved for
another day, but climb the
Tian'an Men *(see p14)* for
the views from the gallery.
From the gate walk east
along the Imperial City
wall soon arriving at an
entrance overlooked by
most visitors: this leads
to the **Imperial Ancestral
Temple**, once one of the
city's most important
places of worship. Carry
on east; after the junction
with Nan Chizi cutting back
inside the wall to walk
through pleasant **Changpu
He Park**. One (long) block
beyond the park is
Wangfujing Dajie and
the Oriental Plaza mall,
with a superb **food court**
in the basement.

Afternoon

Wander up **Wangfujing
Dajie**, making sure to look
in the chopstick and tea
shops. At No. 74 is the
attractive **St. Joseph's
Church**, which is well
worth a look. Immediately
before the church is a
crossroads: head away
from the church along
Deng Shi Kou Jie looking
for signs for Fengfu Hutong
on your right. Here is the
**Former Residence of
Writer Lao She**, offering a
glimpse into a way of life
fast disappearing in Beijing.
Retrace your steps down
Wangfujing to Dong'an
Men Dajie where the
famous **Night Market**
should by now be set up.

Left **Oriental Plaza** Center **Ten Fu's Tea** Right **Foreign Languages Bookstore**

Shops, Malls, and Markets

Oriental Plaza
Several floors of big name international, high-end retailers, from Apple and Sony to Armani and Paul Smith. Don't expect any bargains. ◈ *1 Dong Chang'an Jie • Map N5*

Foreign Languages Bookstore
The whole of the top floor is devoted to English-language fiction and non-fiction. Staff are reliably surly. ◈ *235 Wangfujing Dajie • Map N4*

Ten Fu's Tea
Tea from all over China, sold loose or in beautiful presentation boxes. Staff will brew small cups for sampling. ◈ *88 Wangfujing Dajie • Map N4 • www.tenfu.com*

Sun Dong'an Plaza
A mall full of mid-range clothes shops with a multiscreen cinema and lots of restaurants up on the top floor. ◈ *138 Wangfujing Dajie • Map N4*

Beijing Arts & Crafts Central Store
A vast, multi-story emporium of all kinds of Chinese handicrafts, from cloisonné vases and jade, to wood-carvings, lacquer ware, and silks. ◈ *200 Wangfujing Dajie • Map N4*

Mao's Mausoleum
The mausoleum gift shop is the best source of Mao badges, posters, and shoulder bags. ◈ *Tian'an Men Square • Map L5 • Subway Qian Men • Open 8:30am–11:30am Mon–Sat, 2pm–4pm Mon, Wed & Fri*

Hong Cao Wan'r
Upmarket ladies' clothing boutique specializing in designer oriental items in natural fabrics. ◈ *28 Wangfujing Dajie • Map N3 • Subway: Dengshikou*

Wangfujing Musical Instrument Hall
A whole mall devoted to musical instrument shops. Some of these places are also good for official Chinese releases of foreign CDs, which cost a fraction of what you would pay back home. ◈ *223 Wangfujing Dajie • Map N4*

Jun Yi Home
Chinese military surplus store with badges, patches, and even uniforms. ◈ *383 Dong Si Bei Dajie • Map N2 • Subway Dong Si*

Hao Yuan Market
Small street market just off Wangfujing, which is crammed with stalls selling all manner of knick-knacks, curios, and handicrafts. ◈ *Off Wangfujing Dajie • Map N4*

Most shops, markets, and malls tend to be open approximately 9am–9pm daily. For shopping tips See p111

Price Categories

For the equivalent of a
meal for two made up
of a range of dishes,
served with tea, and
including service.

¥ under ¥100
¥¥ ¥100–¥250
¥¥¥ ¥250–¥500
¥¥¥¥ over ¥500

ove **Wangfujing Night Market**

Restaurants

1 Wangfujing Night Market
A line up of 40 or 50 stalls
tice and repulse in equal
easure with meat kabobs but
so flame-grilled snake and
orpions. ◈ Dong'an Men Dajie
Map M4 • From 5:30pm daily • ¥

2 Oriental Plaza Food Court
The basement of this
scale shopping mall has a
utheast Asian-style food court
ering everything from Chinese
eet foods to sushi. ◈ Corner of
ng Chang'an Jie and Wangfujing Dajie
Map N4 • ¥¥

3 Quanjude
Beijing's most famous duck
staurant has several branches
t this is the most convenient,
st a few steps off southern
angfujing. ◈ 9 Shuai Fu Yuan
tong, Wangfujing Dajie • Map N5
525 3310 • Closes at 9pm • ¥¥

4 Huang Ting
Beautiful recreation of an
d Beijing-style restaurant in
e basement of a five-star hotel
ee p59). ◈ Peninsula
ace Hotel, 8 Jinyu
tong • Map N4 • 8516
38 ext. 6707 • ¥¥¥

5 Made In China
Classy venture
th stunning design
d even better food
ee p58). ◈ Grand
att, 1 Dong Chang'an
• Map N5 • 8518 1234
. 3608 • ¥¥¥

6 My Humble House
High-concept fusion food
in a beautiful conservatory-like
setting next door to the Grand
Hyatt. ◈ W3 West Tower, Oriental Plaza,
1 Dong Chang'an Jie • Map N5 • 8518
8811 • ¥¥¥

7 Princess Mansion
Refined imperial court
cuisine in a mansion that once
belonged to the Empress Cixi.
Excellent food comes with
theatrical frills. ◈ 9 Daqudeng
Hutong, off Meishuguan Hou Dajie
• Map N1 • 6407 8006 • ¥¥¥

8 CourtYard
Beijing's most famous
restaurant – lauded as much for
its location as much as the food
(see p60). ◈ 95 Donghua Men Dajie
• Map M4 • 6526 8883 ext. 6714 • Open
6pm–11:30pm daily • ¥¥¥¥

9 Jing
Outstanding Asian-flavored
fusion menu in refined surrounds
(see p61). ◈ Peninsula Palace Hotel,
8 Jinyu Hutong • Map N4 • 6559 2888
• Open 5:30pm–11:30pm
daily • ¥¥¥¥

10 RBL
Classy, modern
sushi bar (see p61)
with attached blues
bar, Icehouse. ◈ 53 Xi
Pei Building, Dong'an Men
Dajie • Map M4 • 6522
1389 • Open 5:30pm–2am
daily • ¥¥¥¥ • www.rbl-
china.com

Unless otherwise stated, all restaurants are open for lunch and
dinner. Only top-end places accept credit cards

71

Around Town – Tian'an Men Square and the Forbidden City

Left **Natural History Museum** Right **Liulichang Jie**

South of Tian'an Men Square

THE QIAN MEN (FRONT GATE) *at the southern end of Tian'an Men Square was once part of the inner city walls. These divided the imperial quarters of the Manchu emperors from the "Chinese city," where the massed popular lived apart from their overlords. Walking south from the gate you are immediately plunged into a network of narrow and lively* hutongs *(alleys), the remnants of the old quarter. Continuing south down Qian Men Dajie eventually brings you to the western perimeter of the grounds of the Temple of Heaven, one of Beijing's most evocative sights.*

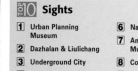

Imperial Vault of Heaven

🔟 Sights

1. Urban Planning Museum
2. Dazhalan & Liulichang
3. Underground City
4. Legation Quarter
5. Temple of Heaven
6. Natural History Museum
7. Ancient Architecture Museum
8. Cow Street Mosque
9. Fayuan Temple
10. South Cathedral

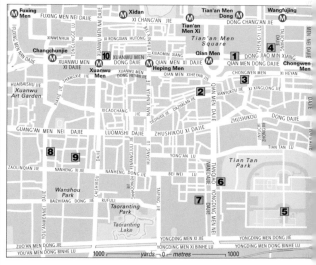

Urban Planning Museum

On display here are dreams the architecture and urban landscape of Beijing to be. These e dramatically represented rough the medium of two ms, plus a vast model that vers most of the third floor, d which is viewable from a llery above. ◈ *Qian Men Dong jie • Map L6 • 6701 7074 • Subway: an Men • 9am–4:30pm Tue–Sun • ¥30*

Dazhalan & Liulichang

Running west off the rthern end of Qian Men Dajie Dazhalan Jie, an old *hutong* ea that is great for exploring on ot or by rickshaw. It is full of uaint Qing-era specialty shops lling pickles, silks, tea, and aditional Chinese medicine. tho west of Dazhalan is ulichang Jie, with more stored buildings and many scinating antique shops. *Map D5–E5 • Subway: Qian Men*

Underground City

At the height of the Sino-oviet rift in the 1960s, Mao edong gave orders to carve out vast network of bombproof nnels beneath Beijing. Part this subterranean hideaway, hich was all built by hand, is en to the public. Guides show sitors around a circuit of dank nnels, where signs illustrate

zhalan Jie

Beijing Police Museum, Legation Quarter

the earlier functions of rooms, variously designated as hospitals armories, and stores for food and water. Unlit passageways branch off from the main corridors, but many are blocked, and it is dangerous to wander off alone. ◈ *62 Xi Damochang Jie • Map M6 • 6702 2657 • Subway: Qian Men • ¥20*

Legation Quarter

When the Conventions of Peking ended the Second Opium War in 1860, foreign delegations were permitted to take up residence in a quarter southeast of the Forbidden City. On main Dong Jiao Min Xiang and surrounding streets, the first modern foreign buildings in Beijing took root. The embassies and Western institutions have long since left and new, mainly governmental occupants moved in, but the architecture left behind is visibly foreign. Two buildings worth visiting are the former City Bank of New York, now the very welcoming Beijing Police Museum *(see p43)*, and St. Michael's Church *(see p47)*. ◈ *Map M5 • Subway: Qian Men • Beijing Police Museum 9am–4pm Tue–Sun*

Temple of Heaven

5 Temple of Heaven
The name refers to a vast complex that encompasses a large, marble sacrificial altar, the iconic three-story Hall of Prayer for Good Harvests, the smaller Imperial Vault of Heaven, and many ancillary buildings, all set in a landscaped park. This is one of Beijing's most absorbing sights. Allow at least a half day to take in everything *(see pp12–13)*.

6 Natural History Museum
An overbearing piece of 1950s architecture houses a great collection of dinosaur skeletons, as well as stuffed pandas and other animals. There are also fish, both dead (preserved in formaldehyde) and alive (in the aquarium). Visitors of

The Boxers

The Boxers, a band of xenophobic rebels from north China who rose up to rid China of the "foreign devils," drew from superstitious rituals that they believed made them invulnerable. Supported by the Empress Dowager Cixi, the rebels laid waste to Beijing's Legation Quarter in 1900 while besieging the district's foreign population. The siege was eventually broken by an eight-power allied force.

a nervous disposition may want to skip the partially dissected human cadavers, also pickled in formaldehyde, which are displayed up on the third floor. ◈ *126 Tangqiao Nan Dajie • Map E6 • 6702 4431 • Subway: Qian Men, then bus • 8:30am–4pm daily • ¥30*

7 Ancient Architecture Museum
Housed in the Hall of Jupiter, part of the Xiannong Tan temple complex, this museum offers an excellent introduction to the ancient construction techniques of Beijing buildings, all helpfully illuminated with detailed models. A fascinating three-dimensional plan shows the city as it was in 1949, with the city walls and gates largely intact. ◈ *21 Dongjing Lu • Map D6 • 6301 7620 • Bus 15 to Nanwei Lu • 9am–4pm daily • ¥15*

8 Cow Street Mosque
Beijing's oldest and largest mosque dates back to the 10th century. It's an attractive building with Islamic motifs and Arabic verses decorating its halls and assorted stelae. Astronomical observations were made from the tower-like Wangyue Lou. The courtyard is lush with greenery, making it an idyllic escape from the city's busy streets. Visitors should dress conservatively, and non-Muslims are not allowed to enter the prayer hall. ◈ *18 Niu Jie • Map C6 • 6353 2564 • Subway: Xuanwu Men, then bus • 8am–sunset daily • ¥1*

Cow Street Mosque

th Cathedral

Fayuan Temple

The Fayuan Temple dates
ck to AD 696 and is probably
e oldest temple in Beijing. All
s time later, it remains a hive
activity. The layout is typical of
ddhist temples. Near the gate,
incense burner is flanked by
 Drum and Bell Towers to the
st and west. Beyond, the Hall
the Heavenly Kings is guarded
a pair of bronze lions. At the
ple's rear, the Scripture Hall
res sutras, while another hall
ntains a 16 ft (5-m) statue of
ddha. ◎ 7 Fayuan Si Qian Jie • Map
• 6353 4171 • Subway: Xuanwu Men,
 bus • 8:30am–3:30pm daily • ¥5

South Cathedral

The first Catholic church
 be built in Beijing stands on
 site of the residence of the
t Jesuit missionary to reach
 city, Matteo Ricci. Arriving in
1, the Italian won the favor of
 Wanli emperor by presenting
 with gifts of European
osities such as clocks and
themathical instruments. Ricci
nded the church in 1605,
ough the present building
es to 1904, replacing a
cture that was burned down
ng the Boxer Rebellion. It
sts some fine stained-glass
dows. ◎ 141 Qian Men Xi Dajie
ap J6 • Subway: Xuanwu Men

A Day South of Tian'an Men Square

Morning

Start on Tian'an Men
Square, at the southeast
corner beside the stripey
brick **Old Qian Men
Railway Station**, built by
the British in 1901, partly
to bring military forces
straight to the assistance
of foreigners in the event
of a repeat of the siege of
the Boxers (see p74). It's
now a shopping mall and
Beijing Opera theater.
Venture east along Dong
Jiao Min Xiang into the
Foreign Legation to visit
the **Police Museum** (see
p43). On leaving head
south to main Qian Men
Dong Dajie and walk back
west for a glimpse of the
Beijing of the future at the
Urban Planning Museum.

From the museum, it is a
short walk south into the
hutongs for a fowl lunch
at the legendary **Liqun
Roast Duck Restaurant**
(see p77).

Afternoon

After eating, if you walk
south you'll hit main
Xianyukou Jie, which,
followed west, becomes
Dazhalan Jie. This is a
great place for specialty
shops. Located down the
first alley on the left is
century-old **Liublju**, selling
a vast array of pickles.
Ruifuxiang, on the north
side of Dazhalan, dates
from 1893 and is renowned
for silks. **Tongrentang
Pharmacy** has been in
business since 1669, while
Zhangyiyuan Chazhuang
has been trading teas since
the early 20th century. At
the end of Dazhalan, head
north up Nan Xinhua Jie to
the **Ji Gu Ge Teahouse**, to
sample more teas in an
atmospheric setting.

Left **Hong Qiao Market** Right **Beijing Silk Store**

⑩ Shops

Hong Qiao Market
A vast indoor market with clothes, bags, shoes, children's toys, plus a basement fish market (see p50). ✆ 36 Hong Qiao Lu • Map F6 • Open 8:30am–7pm daily

Liulichang
Picturesque street renovated in the 1980s to give it that Old China look, but still fun to browse for antiques and art supplies (see p73).

Malian Dao
Beijing's wholesale tea street, with more than 600 tea-shops spread over a mile. Try four-story Tea City (Cha Chang), halfway along the street. ✆ Malian Dao Chayecheng • Map D5

Ruifuxiang
Silk has been sold on this precise spot since 1893. Tailors can make blouses and qipaos (the old-style Chinese dress). ✆ 5 Dazhalan Xijie, off Qian Men Dajie • Map E5 • 6525 0764 • Open 9am–8pm daily

Panjiayuan Antique Market
Set the alarm for dawn for a treasure hunt down at Beijing's sprawling flea market, where anything and everything turns up eventually (see p50). ✆ Panjiayuan Qiao • Map H6 • Subway: Guomao, then taxi • Open 4:30am–2:30pm daily

Beijing Curio City
Just south of Panjiayuan, Curio City has four levels packed with antiques, porcelain, carpet Buddhist statues, jewelry, and furniture. ✆ 21 Dong San Huan Nan • Map H6 • Subway: Guomao, then tax • Open 9:30am–6:30pm daily

Neiliansheng
Beijing's best known shoe store, in business since 1853. Infamous for supplying footwe to Chairman Mao. ✆ 34 Dazhalan • Map E5 • 6301 3037

Beijing Silk Store
Venerable store said to da back to 1840. Prices for quality tailoring, ready-made clothes, and fine cloths are reasonable. ✆ Zhubao Shi 5 • Map L6 • 6301 6658

Yuanlong Silk Company
Hugely popular multi-story emporium specializing in all things silken. ✆ 15 Yongding Men Dong Jie • Map E6 • 6702 2288

Liubiju
A jar of Chinese pickles may not be high on your list of essentials, but a visit to this colorful, 400-year-old shop sho be. ✆ 3 Liangshidian Jie • Map E5

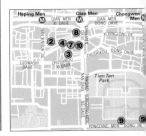

Most shops, markets, and malls tend to be open approximately 9am–9pm daily. For shopping tips **See p111**

...un Roast Duck Restaurant

10 Restaurants and Teahouses

1 Duyichu
Centuries-old corner snack ...op serving *baozi* (steamed ...ns). ◈ *36 Qian Men Dajie • Map L6* ...702 1555 • ¥

2 Lao Beijing Zhajiang Mian Da Wang
...stling institution serving ...ditional Beijing snacks. Kitsch ...t cheap and very tasty fare. ...29 Chongwen Men Wai Dajie • Map ... • 6705 6705 • ¥

3 Fengzeyuan
Specializes in Shandong ...isine, which is heavy on soups ...d seafood. ◈ *83 Zhushikou Xi Dajie* ...Map D5 • 6303 2828 • ¥¥

4 Liqun Roast Duck Restaurant
...king duck at this chaotic, little ...urtyard restaurant is usually ...blime, despite the rough-and-...ady ambience. ◈ *11 Beixianfeng* ...tong, enter from Zhengyi Lu • Map M6 ...705 5578 • ¥¥

5 Qian Men Quanjude
The most famous of the ...anjude restaurants and the ...orse for it. But call by for take-...ay duck pancakes. ◈ *32 Qian* ...n Dajie • Map L6 • 6511 2418 • ¥¥

6 Gongdelin Vegetarian Restaurant
...aranteed meat free, although ...ny dishes feature "mock ...at," which can look like the ...al thing. ◈ *185 Qian Men Nan Dajie* ...Map E5 • 6511 2542 • ¥¥

7 Crab Apple House
A handful of charming, private rooms set around a courtyard garden. Serves light and fragrant Huaiyang cuisine. ◈ *32 Xi Heyan, Xuanwu Men Dong Dajie • Map K6 • 8315 4678 • ¥¥¥*

8 Lao She Teahouse
One of the first in a recent renaissance of old-style Beijing teahouses. Performances of opera and acrobatics take place in a small, upstairs theater. ◈ *3 Qian Men Xi Dajie • Map L6 • 6303 6830 • www.laosheteahouse.com*

9 Ji Gu Ge Teahouse
In addition to tea in all its many kinds and a variety of snacks, the Ji Gu Ge also boasts a small gallery and shop. ◈ *132–6 Liulichang Dong Jie • Map K6 • 6301 7849*

10 Tian Qiao Happy Teahouse
One of the best known teahouses in town. Teas and snacks, plus duck dinners, and nightly Beijing Opera and acrobats. ◈ *Bei Wei Lu, just west of Qian Men Dajie • Map E6 • 6304 0617*

Unless otherwise stated, all restaurants are open for lunch and dinner. Only top-end places accept credit cards

77

Left **Hou Hai bars** Center **Qian Hai** Right **Bell Tower**

North of the Forbidden City

BY FAR THE MOST REWARDING AREA to explore on foot, north of the Forbidden City stretches an almost contiguous run of lakes, either set in parkland or surrounded by swathes of charming historic hutongs. It's an area rich in temple architecture and dotted with grand old courtyard residences. Its appeal to visitors has resulted in restaurants, bars, and shops flooding in to take advantage of the picturesque settings, but thankfully much of the growth has so far been sympathetic.

Mahjong players at Hou Hai

🏮 Sights

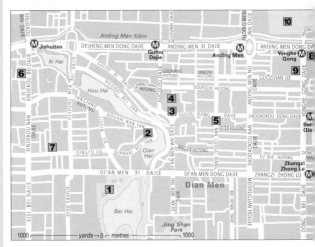

Rickshaws cluster mainly around Qian Hai offering tours around the lakes and hutongs. It's a fine way to see the area See p21

Hai Park

Bei Hai Park

A beautiful example of a classic imperial garden, Bei Hai was a summer playground for successive dynasties that ruled from the neighboring Forbidden City. Today, it is well and truly open to the public, and thronged daily by locals who come here to socialize. There are a couple of small temples, a fine, small ornamental garden, and a noted restaurant. This is arguably the most lovely of Beijing's many fine city parks (see pp18–19).

Hou Hai

The most visitor-friendly neighborhood of Beijing, Hou Hai is three joined lakes surrounded by an expansive and labyrinthine sprawl of age-old *hutongs* (alleys). Visit for a handful of well-preserved mansions, as well as the opportunity to see a more humble form of Beijing life as it has been lived for centuries – but visit soon before the developers have their way and demolish the lot (see pp20–21).

Drum Tower

Drum towers (gu lou) were once found in all major Chinese towns. They housed large drums that were beaten to mark the hour, keeping the city's civil servants on time for work. There has been such a tower on this site since 1272, although the current structure dates to 1420. Visitors can clamber up the torturously steep steps to inspect some 25 drums and be entertained by a troop of drummers that delivers skin-thumping performances on the hour. ⊗ Gulou Dong Dajie • Map E2 • 6401 2674 • Subway: Gulou Dajie • 9am–5pm daily • ¥20

exercise park beside Hou Hai

Confucius

Born in Shandong Province, south of Beijing, during an age of uninterrupted war, Confucius (551–479 BC) was prompted by the suffering around him to develop a practical philosophy built on the principle of virtue. Finding no audience among his native rulers, he embarked on a journey in search of a ruler who would apply his rules of governance. He never found such a person and died unrecognized.

Bell Tower

This dates from 1745 and replaces an earlier tower that burnt down. The great 42-ton (42,674-kg) bell it contains used to be rung to mark the closing of the city gates in the evening. During Spring Festival visitors are allowed to ring the bell for a donation of ¥100. The views from both the Drum and Bell Towers over the neighboring *hutongs* are well worth the exhausting climb. ◈ *Gulou Dong Dajie • Map E1 • 6401 2674 • Subway: Gulou Dajie • 9am–5pm daily • ¥15*

Nan Luogu Xiang

Less than 10 minutes' walk east of the Drum Tower, Nan Luogu Xiang is a lengthy north-south *hutong*. Still traditional in feel, the alley is in the process of receiving a makeover and is now home to several small hotels, as well as a handful of interesting clothing and craft boutiques, and an ever-increasing number of cafés and bars, including the excellent Pass By Bar *(see p82)*. ◈ *Map E2*

Xu Beihong Memorial Museum

Set back from the road with a sign on top in green characters, and opposite a branch of KFC, this museum is dedicated to the man regarded as the founder of modern Chinese painting. It exhibits a collection of the lively watercolors of horses, which made Xu Beihong (1885–1953) internationally famous. ◈ *53 Xinjiekou Bei Dajie • Map D1 • 6225 21 • Subway: Jishuitan • 9am–noon, 1pm–5pm Tue–Sun • ¥10*

Former Residence of Mei Lanfang

This was the home of Beijing Opera's greatest ever performer (1894–1961). The rear rooms have been left with their traditional furniture as it was when he died. Others contain a hagiographic account of his life, as well as diagrams of the stylized movements required by the form and a video of Mei already 61, but still playing the young girl roles for which he was famous *(see p39)*. ◈ *9 Huguosi Ji • Map D2 • 6618 0351 • Subway: Jishuitan • 9am–4pm Tue–Sun • ¥10*

Lama Temple

About a 30-minute walk east of the Drum and Bell Towers, or just a few minutes south of the

Lama Temple

Tan Park

...nghe Gong subway station,
...e Lama Temple is Beijing's
...rgest working temple complex.
...is filled every day with about
... equal number of worshipers
...d visitors *(see pp16–17)*.

Confucius Temple

Just west of the Lama
...mple, the Confucius Temple
...as first built in 1302 during the
...ongol Yuan dynasty, and
...nsiderably expanded in 1906.
...ound 200 ancient stelae stand
...the courtyard in front of the
...ain hall, inscribed with the
...mes of those who success-
...ly passed the imperial civil
...rvice exams. On a marble
...rrace inside the hall are statues
... Confucius and some of his
...sciples. ◈ *13 Guozijian Jie • Map F1*
...402 7224 • Subway: Yonghe Gong •
...0am–4:30pm daily • ¥10

Di Tan Park

The park was named after
...e Temple of Earth (Di Tan),
...ich was a venue for imperial
...crifices. The altar's square
...ape represents the earth.
...ese days, the only thing that
...ts killed here is time: the park
...always full of pensioners
...olling, chatting, and exercising.
...ively temple fair is held here
...Chinese New Year. ◈ *North of*
...na Temple • Map F1 • Subway: Yonghe
...ng • 9am–9pm daily • Park ¥1; Altar ¥5

A Day in the Hutongs

Morning

🕐 Take the subway to Yonghe
Gong for an early morning
– and hopefully crowd-
beating – visit to the **Lama
Temple**. On leaving, cross
over the main road and
pass under the *pailou*
(gate) at the entrance to
Guozijian Jie for the
Confucius Temple.
Afterwards, take a break
at the lovely **Confucius
Teahouse** *(see p59)* over
the road. At the western
end of Guozijian Jie turn
left onto Anding Men Nei
Dajie, a wide, shop-filled
avenue and follow it south
across Jiaodaokou Dong
Dajie and take the first
right into **Ju'er Hutong**,
one of the most vibrant of
the city's old alleys. Take
the first left onto **Nan
Luogu Xiang**, where at
No. 108 you will find the
charming **Pass By Bar**
(see p82), which has a
small courtyard that makes
for an excellent lunchspot.

Afternoon

On leaving the Pass By,
head west along **Mao'er
Hutong** until you reach
main **Di'an Men Wai Dajie**,
where you turn right and
head up the street for the
splendid **Drum and Bell
Towers**. Climb the towers
to pick out the route you've
just taken. Retrace your
steps back down Di'an
Men Wai Dajie taking the
very first right, a tiny
opening (usually marked by
waiting taxis) leading into
bustling **Yandai Xie Jie**.
At the end of this crooked
alley is the **Silver Ingot
Bridge**; cross and bear left
for **Lotus Lane**. You can
stop here for coffee or
head round the southern
tip of the lake to **Han Cang**
(see p83) for a terrific meal
of Hakka cuisine.

Left **Drum & Bell** Right **Pass By Bar**

TOP 10 Bars and Teahouses

1 Bed Tapas & Bar
A short walk north of the Drum and Bell Towers, Bed makes the absolute most of its old courtyard house setting *(see p62)*. ✆ 17 Zhang Wang Hutong, off Jiu Gulou Dajie • Map E1 • 8400 1554

2 Huxley's
The house motto is "Shut up and drink." Compliance is encouraged with cheap beer and cut-price cocktails. ✆ 16 Yandai Xie Jie • Map E2 • 6402 7825 • 6pm–late daily

3 Lotus Bar
Another fine Yandai Xie Jie bar, this one squeezed into a narrow, two-story house with a compact, boho interior and roof terrace. ✆ 29 Yandai Xie Jie • Map E2 • 6407 7857

4 Drum & Bell
A modest bar in the shadow of antiquity offering refreshment and a gentle respite from sightseeing *(see p62)*. ✆ 41 Zhong Lou Wan Hutong • Map E2 • 8403 3600

5 Guan Tang
Cozy bar with a tranquil atmosphere, although with cocktails at just ¥30 things often don't stay that tranquil for long. ✆ 13 Dongming Hutong • Map E2

6 No Name Bar
The perfect lakeside drinking den. Expect stiff competition from the house cat for the best seats *(see p62)*. ✆ 3 Qianhai Dongyan • Map E2 • 6401 8541

7 Pass By Bar
It may be book-filled but the atmosphere is anything but hushed at this lending library-cum-café/bar *(see p62)*. ✆ 108 N. Luogu Xiang • Map E2 • 8403 8004

8 East Shore Live Jazz Café
Opened by legendary jazzman Liu Yuan. Climb steep wooden stairs to four walls of floor-to-ceiling windows and a roof terrace, plus live music. ✆ Qianhai Nanyan Lu • Map E2 • 8403 21

9 Xin Bar
This little gem has colorful Yunnan decorations, leafy foliag and a roof terrace overlooking the surrounding *hutongs*. As w as cheap beer there are ten typ of tea. ✆ 152 Jiu Gulou Dajie • Map • 6400 7571

10 Jia Fu Teahouse
Modeled after a Qing-era home, this teahouse is filled w antique furniture and often has live Chinese music. ✆ Hou Hai N Yan • Map E2 • 6616 0725

Unless otherwise stated bars are generally open from around noon until 2am

Price Categories

For the equivalent of a meal for two made up of a range of dishes, served with tea, and including service.

¥	under ¥100
¥¥	¥100–¥250
¥¥¥	¥250–¥500
¥¥¥¥	over ¥500

t **Han Cang** Center **Raj**

10 Restaurants

1 Fish Nation
Enterprising venture serving English-style fish and chips to bar crawlers. ◈ *31 Nan Luogu Xiang* • *Map E2* • *6401 3249* • *¥*

2 Cafe Sambal
An old-style courtyard house serves as the venue for exquisite dishes prepared by a genuine Malaysian chef *(see p60)*. ◈ *43 Dufuchi Hutong, off Jiu Gulou Dajie* • *Map E1* • *6400 4875* • *¥¥*

3 Han Cang
Bustling two-story rustic restaurant with a large outdoor dining area always packed with locals enjoying simple, tasty Hakka dishes *(see p58)*. ◈ *Ping'an Dao* • *Map E2* • *6404 2259* • *¥¥*

4 Kaorou Ji
Majors in Qingzhen cuisine, which means mutton and more mutton. The house specialty is spiced barbecued lamb and sesame seed bread. ◈ *14 Qianhai Dong Yan* • *Map E2* • *6404 2554* • *¥¥*

5 Kong Yiji
Lakeside restaurant with an enormous range of exquisite dishes from the Yangzi River delta. ◈ *Desheng Men Nei Dajie* • *Map* • *6618 4917* • *¥¥*

6 Nuage
Well-respected Vietnamese with lovely location just south of the Silver Ingot Bridge *(see p61)*. ◈ *22 Qian Hai Dong Yan* • *Map E2* • *6401 ?1* • *¥¥*

7 Raj
Cheap and authentic south Indian cuisine. The décor is kitsch but there's a pleasant outdoor terrace. ◈ *31 Gulou Xidajie* • *Map E1* • *6401 1675* • *¥¥*

8 South Silk Road
Spicy Yunnanese food in stylish surroundings beside the lakes *(see p59)*. ◈ *19A Lotus Lane* • *Map E2* • *6615 5515* • *¥¥*

9 Mei Fu
The setting is a gorgeous courtyard house lavishly filled with antiques. Set menus of sweet and rich Shanghainese cuisine start from ¥200 per person. ◈ *24 Daxiangfeng Hutong* • *Map D2* • *6612 6845* • *¥¥¥*

10 Li Family Imperial Cuisine
Intimate courtyard restaurant serving imperial court cuisine. Set menus range from ¥200 to ¥1,500 a head but the food is exquisite. ◈ *11 Yangfang Hutong* • *Map D2* • *6618 0107* • *4:30pm–10pm daily* • *¥¥¥/¥¥¥¥*

Unless otherwise stated, all restaurants are open for lunch and dinner. Only top-end places accept credit cards

83

Left **Sanlitun bar** Right **Red Gate Gallery at the Southeast Corner Watchtower**

Eastern Beijing

EAST OF CENTRAL BEIJING, *in a corridor between the Second and Third Ring Roads, is the district of Chaoyang. It's not an area that is particular old and it doesn't have very many significant monuments, but it is home to two main clusters of international embassies, and it is where a large proportion of the city's foreign expatriate community chooses to live. As a result, Chaoyang is the city's entertainment and nightlife center, and, for the visitor, it is the prime area for eating and shopping.*

🔟 Sights

1. Ancient Observatory
2. Southeast Corner Watchtower
3. Ri Tan Park
4. SOHO
5. Dong Yue Miao
6. Blue Zoo Beijing
7. Workers' Stadium
8. Sanlitun
9. Ghost Street
10. Lufthansa Center

Crowds at the Workers' Stadium

Ri Tan Park

Distances in eastern Beijing are considerable and it may be preferable to take taxis between some of the sights

Ancient Observatory

Ancient Observatory

Dating to 1442, Beijing's observatory is one of the oldest [in] the world. In fact, there was an even earlier Yuan-dynasty (1279–1368) observatory also located [on] this site but no trace of that remains. Today, a collection of reproduction astronomical devices lies in the courtyard, some decorated with fantastic Chinese designs. There are more impressive instruments on the roof. ◈ Map G4 • 6524 2202 • Subway: [Ji]anguo Men • 9am–5pm daily • ¥10

Southeast Corner Watchtower

[A] short distance south of the [S]econd Ring Road an imposing [ch]unk of the old Beijing city [w]all survives, including an [im]posing 15th-century watch[to]wer. Visitors can climb onto [th]e battlements and walk along [a] short stretch of wall. The tower [is] also home to the commercial [Re]d Gate Gallery (see p49). ◈ South of Jianguo Men Nei Dajie • Map [G]5 • 6527 0574 • Subway: Jianguo Men [9]am–5:30pm daily • ¥10

Ri Tan Park

One of the city's oldest parks, Ri Tan was laid out around a sacrificial altar back in the 16th century. The round altar remains, ringed by a circular wall, but this is very much a living park, filled daily with people walking and exercising. Being at the heart of the embassy district, the park is well tended and surrounded by lots of good restaurants and cafés. ◈ Guanghua Lu • Map G4 • 8561 4261 • Subway: Jianguo Men • 6:30am–9:30pm daily

SOHO

Beijing's own SOHO (it stands for Small Office, Home Office) is a high-rise complex of residential and commercial property in the city's rapidly developing Central Business District. It represents a new form of Chinese design, somewhere between Scandinavian modern and Ming minimalism. Visit to see what some believe represents the future of Beijing, also for good shopping, dining, and for the chance to meet real Chinese yuppies. ◈ South of Jianguo Men Wai Dajie • Map H4 • Subway: Guomao

Southeast Corner Watchtower

For more modern architecture in eastern Beijing See pp40–41

Altared city

Ri Tan Park's Altar of the Sun is one of eight such cosmologically aligned structures, along with the Altar of Heaven (Tian Tan; *see pp12–13*), the Altar of Agriculture (Xiannong Tan; now part of the Ancient Architecture Museum; *see p74*), the Altar of the Moon in the west of the city, the Altar of the Earth (Di Tan, *see p81*), the Altar of the Country in Zhong Shan Park, the Altar of the Silkworm in Bei Hai Park, and the lost Altar of the Gods of Heaven.

Dong Yue Miao

This colorful and active temple, dating to the early 14th century, was restored in 1999 and is tended by Daoist monks. The main courtyard leads into the Hall of Tai Shan with statues of gods and their attendants. Tai Shan is another name for Dong Yue, in Daoist lore the Eastern peak to which the spirits of the dead travel. 🕲 *141 Chaoyang Men Wai Dajie • Map G3 • 6551 0151 • Subway: Chaoyang Men • 8:30am–4:30pm Tues–Sun • ¥10*

Dong Yue Miao

Blue Zoo Beijing

Not a zoo at all, but an excellent modern aquarium, reckoned to be the best of its kind in Asia. The main attraction is a central tank holding literally thousands of fish, plus there are also 18 additional tanks with specifically themed displays *(see p53)*. 🕲 *South gate of Workers' Stadium • Map G3 • 6591 3397 ext. 1560*

• *Subway: Chaoyang Men • 8am–8pm daily • ¥75; children ¥50; under 3 ft (1 m) free • www.blue-zoo.com*

Workers' Stadium

With an estimated capacity of 72,000, the stadium is home to Beijing's premier football club Hyundai Guo'an, and it is the city's main venue for large-scale rock and pop concerts. Perplexingly, it's also a hub of Beijing nightlife, with numerous clubs and bars clustered around its north and west gates, and some very good restaurants too *(see p89)*. Even oldies get in on the act, with mass open-air dancing taking place on the forecourt of the north gate most summer evenings. 🕲 *Gongren Tiyuchang Bei Lu • Map G2 • 6501 2372 • Subway: Dong Si Shi Tiao*

Sanlitun

Beijing's main expat-friendly boozing district, Sanlitun is famed for its "Bar Street", more properly known as Sanlitun Bei Lu. It also has the highest concentration of decent international restaurants *(see p89)* and lots of boutique shopping *(see p88)*. Streets around here, although modern, are at least tree-lined and, with plenty of cafés for refreshment stops, it's a pleasant district in which to wander. 🕲 *Map H2 • Subway: Dong Si Shi Tiao*

Entrance gate at the Workers' Stadium

Sanlitun's Na Li Market

Ghost Street

Gui Jie, or Ghost Street, is a mile-and-a-quarter (2-km) stretch of Dong Zhi Men Nei Dajie that come nightfall is jammed with cars double-parked outside its string of around one hundred or so restaurants, many of which open 24 hours. The roadside is all festively lit with strings of red lanterns bobbing in the breeze, while most establishments favor corny, old-China décor with lots of red lacquer and pagoda motifs, and waitresses in silk tunics. This is the home of hotpot, though all regional Chinese cuisines are represented here.
● Map F2 • Subway: Dong Zhi Men

Lufthansa Center

This glossy mall-style development caters for aspirational Beijingers with a department store full of imported luxury goods, a basement continental deli, and a BMW showroom. More down to earth, just west on the south bank of the river is the Liang Ma Flower Market, which is a riot of color and fragrances. ● 50 Liang Ma Qiao Lu • Map H1 • 6465 1188 • Subway: Dong Zhi Men • Open 9am–10pm daily

A Walk From Ri Tan Park to Sanlitun

Morning

The American-style diner **Steak and Eggs** (5 Xiushui Jie), which is behind the Friendship Store, opens for pancake-platter breakfasts at 7:30am. Well fed, head north up embassy-lined Jianhua Lu to enter **Ri Tan Park** via the south gate. This is one of the city's best parks, with an old sacrificial altar, a rockery, and a small lake with the waterside **Stone Boat** café. Exit via the west gate onto Ritan Lu, which is lined by shops with signs in Cyrillic. This area is **Yabao Lu**, Beijing's Russian neighborhood. Walk north to **Aliens Street Market**, a two-story jumble of cheap clothing, shoes, and cosmetics. Continue on to the next major junction and turn right on to busy Chaoyang Men Wai Dajie, lined with malls and the **Dong Yue Miao** temple.

Afternoon

Departing the temple, turn left and then take the second left into Gongren Lu. This takes you up to a park with a lake and then the **Workers' Stadium**. Circle the stadium to exit via the north gate onto Gongren Tiyuchang Bei Lu. Head east until you come to a foot bridge, which allows you to cross this eight-lane boulevard safely. It deposits you in front of **Yaxiu Market** for more bargain shopping. Continue east until Sanlitun Bei Lu, the heart of the city's entertainment district: bars **The Tree** (see p63) and **Bookworm** (see p61), plus restaurant **Alameda** (see p89) are all just a few minute's walk from here.

Left **Sunglasses at the Silk Market** Center **Boots at Yaxiu Market** Right **Na Li Market**

Shops, Markets, and Malls

Silk Market
It can't last, but for the time being this four-story indoor market remains the lodestone for counterfeit designer goods. Don't forget to haggle as if your life depended on it *(see p50).* ⊗ *Jianguo Men Wai Dajie • Map G4*

Yaxiu Market
Similar to the Silk Market, but significantly less crowded *(see p50).* ⊗ *58 Gongren Tiyuchang Bei Lu • Map H2 • 6415 1726*

China World Shopping Mall
The Silk Market and Yaxiu Market sell the counterfeits, but this is where you come for the originals *(see p51).* ⊗ *1 Jianguo Men Wai Dajie • Map H4*

Na Li Market
A small dead-end lane off the southern end of Bar Street with a string of small clothing and jewelry boutiques that mix fakes with one-offs by young, local designers. Hip, but also reasonably priced. ⊗ *Sanlitun Bei Lu • Map H2*

Friendship Store
Once upon a time this was officially the only store tourists could visit. Now it's the last place you'd want to shop; it's overpriced and has notoriously unhelpful staff. Visit instead for a glimpse of how shopping in Beijing was in the good old bad old days. ⊗ *17 Jianguo Men Wai Dajie • Map G4 • 6500 3311*

Dong Jiao Wholesale Market
This is where the traders from Beijing's other markets come to buy their stock *(see p51).* ⊗ *Dong Si Huan Zhong Lu • Map G4*

Ri Tan Office Building
A former office building on the south side of Ri Tan Park, now a warren of small, independent boutiques. ⊗ *15A Guanghua Lu • Map G4 • 8561 9556*

Aliens Street Market
Another in the same mold as the Silk Market, but with a pronounced Slavic twist *(see p51).* ⊗ *Yabao Lu • Map G3*

Tong Li Studios
Four floors of independent designer clothing and decorative arts stores, plus jewelry and hip cafés, and up on the top floor a couple of lively bars. One block west of Bar Street. ⊗ *Sanlitun Bei Lu • Map H2*

Jenny Lou's
Expat heaven with genuine Dutch cheese, German sausage, French wines, and such like ⊗ *4 Ri Tan Bei Lu • Map G3 • 8563 0626*

Price Categories

For the equivalent of a meal for two made up of a range of dishes, served with tea, and including service.

¥	under ¥100
¥¥	¥100–¥250
¥¥¥	¥250–¥500
¥¥¥¥	over ¥500

ve **Hatsune**

Restaurants

Beijing Dadong Roast Duck Restaurant

s the opinion of a great many ijingers that there is no finer ck than that served here *(see 8).* Bdg 3, Tuanjiehu Beikou, Dong Huan • Map H2 • 6582 2892 • ¥

Three Guizhou Men

Test your taste buds on the es of sour fish soup and a rtling take on ribs and mashed tato *(see p58).* 6 Guanghua Xili Map G4 • 6502 1733 • ¥

Afunti

A Xinjiang restaurant, which eans lamb kabobs, flat breads, s live bands and the inevitable dience participation. It may be risty but it's fun *(see p59).* 188 Denei Dajie, Chaoyang Men Nei ic • Map F3 • 6527 2288 • ¥¥

Bellagio

Packed until the early hours h hip Beijingers filling up on bs before moving on to one the clubs up the street *(see 3).* 6 Gongren Tiyuchang Xi Lu • o G2 • 6551 3533 • ¥¥

Guizhou Luo Luo Suan ng Yu

host Street" is un place to dine, d this hotpot ecialist is one of best eateries *(see 3).* 186 Dong Zhi n Nei Dajie • Map F2 405 1717 • ¥¥

Alameda

Beautiful modern restaurant serving Brazilian-inspired contemporary cuisine *(see p60).* Na Li Market, off Sanlitun Bei Lu • Map H2 • 6417 8084 • ¥¥¥

Hatsune

A class act: stylish Japanese restaurant with fresh fish flown in daily *(see p60).* 2nd floor, Heqiao Building C, 8a Guanghua Dong Lu • Map H4 • 6581 3939 • ¥¥¥

Morel's

Beijing's sole Belgian restaurant is a big expat favorite for steak and seafood, including, of course, mussels, as well as a great range of Belgian beers *(see p61).* Gongren Tiyuchang Bei Lu, Chunxiu Lu • Map G2 • 6416 8802 • ¥¥¥

Aria

The Continental-Asian fusion cuisine here constitutes possibly the most satisfying dining experience in Beijing *(see p60).* China World Hotel, 1 Jianguo Men Wai Dajie • Map H4 • 6505 2266 • ¥¥¥¥

Green T. House

Gimmick or culinary wonder? Make your own mind up, but certainly take a look at Beijing's most jaw-dropping, China-meets-Alice-in-Wonderland interior *(see p60).* 6 Gongren Tiyuchang Xi Lu • Map G2 • 6552 8311 • ¥¥¥¥

Unless otherwise stated, all restaurants are open for lunch and dinner. Only top-end places accept credit cards

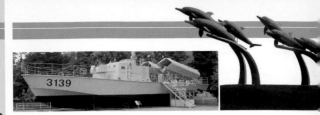

Left **Chinese Military History Museum** Right **Beijing Aquarium**

Western Beijing

XICHENG, WHICH IN CHINESE MEANS "WEST CITY", *is the central district west of the Forbidden City and the lakes. It's an area that lacks any great landmarks, and neither is it pedestrian-friendly in the way that Hou Hai or the Sanlitun areas are. It is best experienced as a series of half-day expeditions: a visit to the Military Museum with a look at the Millennium Monument afterwards and a walk through Yuyuan Tan Park, or a trip to the zoo and aquarium followed by the Temple of the Five Pagodas. Expect to make liberal use of taxis and the subway.*

Temple of the Five Pagodas

Millennium Monument

🔟 Sights

1. Temple of Heavenly Tranquility
2. White Clouds Temple
3. Chinese Military History Museum
4. Millennium Monument
5. Miaoying Temple White Dagoba
6. Lu Xun Museum
7. Beijing Exhibition Hall
8. Beijing Zoo
9. Beijing Aquarium
10. Temple of the Five Pagodas

1 Temple of Heavenly Tranquility

ome to Beijing's most
iking pagoda, the temple
anning Si) was
ilt during the
h century AD,
aking it one of
e city's oldest.
e 196-ft (60-m)
tagonal pagoda
as added in the
rly 12th century.

Temple of Heavenly Tranquility

e bottom of the pagoda is
the form of a huge pedestal
corated with carved arch
tterns, symbolizing Sumeru,
e mountain of the gods. Above
e thirteen levels of eaves, very
ose together, with no doors or
ndows – the pagoda is with-
t stairs inside or outside and
in fact, solid. ◈ *Guang'an Men
nbinhe Lu • Map B5 • Subway:
nlishi Lu, then taxi*

2 White Clouds Temple

The first temple on this
e was founded in AD 739 and
rnt down in 1166. Since that
ne, it has been repeatedly
stroyed and rebuilt. It even
rvived being used as a factory
ring the Cultural Revolution.
e shrines, pavilions, and
urtyards that make up the
mpound today date mainly
m the Ming and Qing
nasties. Monks here are
owers of Daoism and
ort distinctive top-
ots. Each Chinese
w Year this is the
nue for one of the
y's most popular
nple fairs, with
rformers, artisans,
d traders. ◈ *6 Baiyun
an Jie, off Lianhuachi Dong
• Map B4 • 6340 4812 •
oway: Nanlishi Lu • 8:30am–
0pm daily • ¥10*

3 Chinese Military History Museum

Vast halls of Cold War-era
hardware including lots of
silvery fighter planes
and tanks fill the
ground floor.
Upstairs has
exhibitions on
historic conflicts,
including the
Opium Wars and
Boxer Rebellion.
Unfortunately, there is little
labeling in English. What is not
mentioned is that the museum is
close to the Muxidi intersection,
scene of a massacre of civilians
by the Chinese army during the
1989 democracy protests.
◈ *9 Fuxing Lu • Map A4 • 6686 6244
• Subway: Junshi Bowuguan • 8am–
5:30pm daily • ¥5*

4 Millennium Monument

Built to welcome the year
2000, Beijing's millennial
structure is a curious bit of
concrete constructivism that
looks like something that might
have adorned Moscow back in
the 1920s. It is fashioned to
resemble a giant tilted sundial.
Inside is a plaza with the "Holy
Fire of China" (a flame fed on
natural gas), plus several
exhibition halls. ◈ *9 Yuyuan Tan
Nan Lu • Map A4 • 6686 6244 • Subway:
Junshi Bowuguan • 8:30am–4:30pm daily*

Gateway at the White Clouds Temple

*There are few good restaurants in Western Beijing but Hou Hai, with
its excellent dining, is only a short taxi ride away* **See p83**

Buddhism in China

Buddhism, which started in India, probably came to China along the Silk Route. The earliest sign of the religion is associated with the founding of the White Horse Temple near the old capital of Luoyang in AD 68. Buddhism surged in popularity during periods of instability, when Confucianism's veneration for authority did not sit well with the populace. It was eventually adopted by China's rulers.

Miaoying Temple White Dagoba monks

5 Miaoying Temple White Dagoba

Celebrated for its Tibetan-styled, 167-ft (51-m) white *dagoba* (stupa), said to have been designed by a Nepalese architect, the temple dates to 1271, when Beijing was under Mongol rule. The temple is also noted for its fascinating collection of thousands of Tibetan Buddhist statues. ✪ *171 Fucheng Men Nei Dajie • Map C3 • 6616 0211 • Subway: Fucheng Men • 9am–4pm daily • ¥10*

6 Lu Xun Museum

Lu Xun is regarded as the father of modern Chinese literature, responsible for ground-breaking works such as "Diary of a Madman" and "The True Story of Ah Q". This is the house in which he lived from 1924 to 1926. The rooms display artifac relating to his life and there's also an adjacent exhibition hall with more than 10,000 letters, journals, photographs, and othe personal objects. ✪ *19 Gong Men Kou Er Tiao, off Fucheng Men Nei Dajie Map C3 • 6616 4168 • Subway: Fucher Men • 9am–4pm Tues–Sun*

7 Beijing Exhibition Hall

A monument to the one-time ideological union betweer China and the USSR, the hall is a Muscovite-styled period piec (built 1954) fronted by a red-sta topped spire. Although not generally open to the public yo can usually access the entranc lobby, which is festooned with massive crystal chandeliers. ✪ *138 Xizhi Men Wai Dajie • Map B2 • 6831 2517 • Subway: Xizhi Men*

8 Beijing Zoo

Visit for the pandas, the famously rare bears that are native to China and nowhere else. The zoo has several, housed in a new "panda house However, most of the other 2,000 animals here are not so lucky; their cages are tiny. ✪ *137 Xizhi Men Wai Dajie • Map B2 • 6831 4411 • Subway: Xizhi Men • 7:30am–5:30pm daily • ¥10, pandas ¥5 extra*

9 Beijing Aquarium

Located in the northeaster corner of the zoo is this new and very impressive addition. It's reputedly the largest inland aquarium in the world, with massive tanks containing thousands of weird and wonderful fish, plus a shark ta coral reefs and an "Amazon rainforest." There are also seve dolphin and seal shows held

ing Aquarium

roughout the day. ◈ *108 Gao ng Qiao Xijie • Map B2 • 6217 6655 am–5pm daily • ¥100 adults, ¥50 dren • www.bj-sea.com*

Temple of the Five Pagodas

st north of the zoo, this mple displays obvious Indian luences. It was built in the rly 15th century in honor of an dian monk who came to China d presented the emperor with e golden Buddhas. The godas sport elaborate carvings curvaceous females, as well the customary Buddhas. Also re is the Beijing Art Museum Stone Carvings, with 2,000 corative stelae. ◈ *24 Wuta Si Cun Map B1 • 6217 3836 • Subway: Xizhi n • 9am–4pm Mon–Sun • ¥10*

mple of the Five Pagodas

War and peace

Morning

🕐 Even if you're no big fan of mechanized heavy armor, the **Chinese Military History Museum** is a fascinating place to spend a morning. Exhibits begin with the technology that made China one of the world's first military superpowers, including the "Flying Dragon," an early form of missile launcher. There's one room devoted to the wonderfully tacky gifts that have been bestowed on China's army chiefs and leaders, such as a pistol presented to Chairman Mao by Fidel Castro. Mao's limousine is displayed on the ground floor and there's one hall devoted to statues and assorted representations of the Communist Party's great and good. It all makes for a fascinating insight into the mentality of late 20th-century China.

Afternoon

Leaving the museum, turn right and walk west along Fuxing Lu and take the first right; this will bring you to the **Millennium Monument** *(see p91)*. One of the oddest bits of architecture in Beijing, the Monument nevertheless plays an active role in the city's cultural life; its various halls are used for all kinds of temporary exhibitions. There is almost always something worth seeing. Afterwards, for some refreshment, walk east to the very pleasant 🍵 **Hong Hao Ge Teahouse** *(see p59)*. North of the teahouse stretches the vast and very green **Yuyuan Tan Park**, with a large lake at its center. It makes for a relaxing place to stroll.

Left **Marble Boat, Summer Palace** Right **798 Art District**

Greater Beijing

B EIJING IS VAST. *Although you could spend all your time without ever straying too far from the area around central Tian'an Men Square, you would be missing out on a lot. Way out in the northwest of the city is a clus of sights that includes the unmissable Summer Palace, with the almost equally intoxicating hillside Xiang Shan Park and the haunting ruins of the Yuanming Yuan, or Old Summer Palace, close by. It might be a squeeze to get all three into one day's sightseeing but it's worth a try. For fans of contemporary urban culture, the 798 Art District in the northeast of the city is an absolute must, and you can drop in on the markets and bars of Nuren Jie on the way back into town.*

TOP 10 Sights

1 Summer Palace

2 Yuanming Yuan (Old Summer Palace)

3 Xiang Shan Park

4 Great Bell Temple

5 Beijing Botanical Gardens

6 China Ethnic Culture Park

7 Science and Technology Museum

8 Nuren Jie

9 798 Art District

10 Railway Museum

Bronze ox, Summer Palace

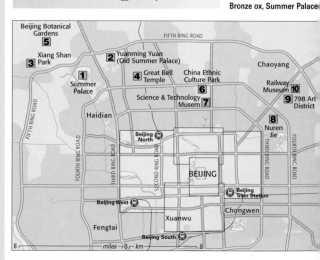

g Corridor ceiling, Summer Palace

Summer Palace

It's a long 45-minute taxi
e from central Beijing to the
mmer Palace, but it is a
ht that should not be
ssed. The grounds are
anged as a microcosm
nature, with hills and
ter complemented by
dges, temples and
lkways. It manages to
both fanciful and
rmonious at the same
e *(see pp18–19).*

Yuanming Yuan (Old Summer Palace)

e name Yuanming Yuan derives
m a Buddhist term and can be
nslated as "Garden of Perfect
ghtness". This was the largest
d most elaborate of
the summer
aces of the Qing
. It once contained
vate imperial
idences, pleasure
vilions, Buddhist
nples, a vast
perial ancestral
rine, pools for
dfish, and canals
d lakes for pleasure
ating. The Qianlong
peror even added a
up of European-

style palaces designed by Jesuit
missionary-artists serving in the
Qing court. Today, all that's left
are graceful, fragmentary ruins
after the complex was razed to
the ground during the Second
Opium War (1856–1860). A small
museum displays images and
models of the place as it was.
⊛ 28 Qinghua Xi Lu • 6262 8501
• Subway: Xizhi Men, then bus 375
• 7am–7pm daily • ¥10

Xiang Shan Park

The wooded parkland area,
also known as Fragrant Hills
Park, is 2 miles (3 km) west of
the Summer Palace. It boasts
fine views from Incense Burner
Peak, which is accessible
by a chair lift (¥30). Close
to the park's main gate is
the Azure Clouds Temple
(Biyun Si), guarded by the
menacing deities Heng
and Ha in the Mountain
Gate Hall. A series of
farther halls leads to the
Sun Yat Sen Memorial Hall,
where the revolutionary
leader's coffin was stored
in 1925, before being taken
to his final resting place
in Nanjing. ⊛ Wofosi Lu • 6259 1155
• Bus: 333 from Summer Palace, 360
from Beijing Zoo • 6am–7pm daily • ¥5;
Azure Clouds Temple ¥10

Guardian deity, Heng

Yuanming Yuan (Summer Palace)

Great Bell Temple
The 18th-century Da Zhong Si follows a typical Buddhist plan, with a Heavenly Kings Hall, Main Hall, and a Guanyin Bodhisattva Hall. What distinguishes it, though, is the 46.5 ton (47, 250 kg) bell – one of the world's largest – that is housed in the rear tower. The bell was cast between 1403 and 1424 and Buddhist *sutras* in Chinese and Sanskrit cover its surface. Hundreds more bells can be seen in another hall on the west side of the complex.
⊗ *31A Beisanhuan Xi Lu • Map B1 • 6254 1971 • Bus: 300, 367 • 8:30am–4pm daily • ¥10*

Beijing Botanical Gardens
About a mile (2 km) northeast of Xiang Shan Park lie these pretty gardens, containing some 3,000 plant species and some pleasant walks. The garden's Sleeping Buddha Temple (Wofo Si) is renowned for its magnificent 15-ft (5-m) bronze statue of a reclining Buddha. China's last emperor, Pu Yi *(see p9)*, ended his days here as a gardener.
⊗ *6259 1283 • Bus: 333 from Summer Palace, 360 from Beijing Zoo • 6am–7pm daily • ¥5*

China Ethnic Culture Park
A theme park devoted to all 55 of China's ethnic minorities *(see box)*, the complex is crammed with a weird and

China Ethnic Culture Park

wonderful array of buildings such as the distinctive circular dwellings of the southern Hakka people, some of which are full-size replicas, while others are scale models. There is also a Chinese Song and Dance Theater featuring daily performances by ethnic representatives in full costume. If you aren't going to be traveling around the country this is a fine way to get an idea the diversity of China. ⊗ *1 Minzu Yuan Lu • Map E1 • 6206 3640 • Subway Gan Yang Shu • 8am–6pm daily • ¥60*

Science and Technology Museum
Exhibits begin with ancient science, highlighting China's "technological pre-eminence in history." The technology comes up to date with Chinese space capsules, robots, and an Astro-vision Theater incorporating state-of-the-art cinematography. Although this museum opened only in 1988, a new science museum is already under construction and is due to open in time for the 2008 Olympics.
⊗ *1 Beisanhuan Zhong Lu • Map E1 • 6237 1177 • 9am–4:30pm Tue–Sat • ¥3*

Nuren Jie
"Women's Street" is a relatively undeveloped area just north of the Lufthansa Center *(see p87)* and Kempinski Hotel between the Third and Fourth

China's Peoples
There are about 55 different ethnic minorities in China, each with their own distinctive customs and, in may cases, languages. Though rich in culture, and varied, together they make up only seven percent of the population, with the main group, known as Han Chinese, accounting for the rest.

ng Roads. It's where to shop
flowers and tropical fish at
 Lai Tai Market *(see p51)* and
 cheap mobiles at the Grand
rld Electrical Market *(see
1)*. There's also a lively nightlife
eet here, home to the New
t Lucky music bar *(see p63)*
ong others. ◈ *Off Xiaoyun Lu
Map H1*

798 Art District
Although it's called the
8 Art District, Factory number
8 is only one of a number of
mer industrial units that have
en taken over by artists and
leries to form what is often
erred to as Beijing's answer to
w York's Meatpacking District
e pp24–5).

China Railway Museum
The last passenger steam
vices in China came to an
d in 2006, but a short taxi
e northeast of the 798 Art
strict is this new museum
h a sizeable collection of old
omotives. Some of the cabs
 be boarded. An exhibition
 the history of China's railways
romised and some of the
chines will occasionally be
steam. In the meantime, the
gines are a must for small
ys of all ages. ◈ *1 Jiuxian Qiao
Lu • Map H1 • 6438 1317 • 9am–4pm
–Sun • ¥20*

na Railway Museum

Green Beijing

Morning
🕗 Be at the East Gate (Dong
Men) of the **Summer
Palace** for 8:30am to beat
both the heat (if you are
visiting in summer) and
the crowds. Make your
way along the north shore
of Kunming Lake via the
Long Corridor and ascend
Longevity Hill. Descend
again to the Marble Boat
and take a pleasure cruiser
across the lake to **South
Lake Island**. Cross back
to the mainland via the
supremely elegant
Seventeen-arch Bridge;
from here it's a short walk
north to exit where you
came in at the East Gate.
In the car park pick up a
taxi and instruct the driver
to take you to **Xiang Shan
Gongyuan**, otherwise
known as Fragrant Hills
Park. Before you enter,
🍴 **Sculpting In Time** is a
café near the East Gate
that does good salads,
pastas, and pizza.

Afternoon
From the park's East Gate
turn right for the **Temple
of Brilliance**, built in 1780
and ransacked by Western
troops in 1860 and 1900.
Close by is the **Liuli
Pagoda**, with bells hanging
from its eaves that chime
in the breeze. Continue
north to pass between two
small round lakes linked by
a small hump-backed
bridge – the whole known
as the **Spectacles Lakes**.
Beyond is a **chair lift** that
takes you up to the top of
the "Fragrant Hill". Zigzag
back down past many more
pavilions to arrive at the
🏨 **Fragrant Hills Hotel**,
designed by Chinese-
American architect I.M.
Pei, otherwise best known
for his glass pyramid at the
Louvre in Paris.

Left **Marco Polo Bridge** Right **Great Palace Gate, Ming Tombs**

Trips Out of Town

B EIJING HAS MORE THAN ENOUGH SIGHTS *to keep the average visitor busy, but after traveling all this way, it would be a shame not to grasp the opportunity to get out of the city. Of course, the Great Wall is an absolut must, but not far from the city are also ancient temples nestled on green hillsides and the vast necropolises of the Ming and Qing emperors. To the southwest is the 300-year-old stone Marco Polo Bridge and neighboring Wanping, a rare surviving example of a walled city. Both are an easy suburban bus ride from the city. Otherwise, most Beijing hotels organize tours to these sights.*

Spirit Way at the Ming Tombs

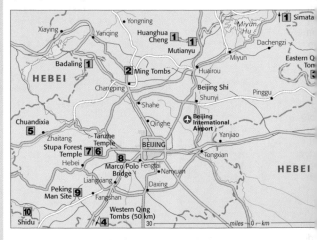

The Great Wall, snaking over high ridges north of Beijing

Great Wall

A visit to the wall is an absolute must. The closest section to Beijing is at Badaling, and you can get there and back in half a day. However, if you suspect that your appreciation of this matchless monument would be improved by the absence of coach-loads of fellow tourists, then considering traveling that little bit farther to the sites at Mutianyu, Huanghua Cheng, and Simatai *(see pp28–9)*.

Ming Tombs

The Ming Tombs are the resting place for 13 of the 16 Ming emperors. These are Confucian shrines and follow a standard layout of a main gate leading to a series of courtyards and a main hall, with a "soul tower" and burial mound beyond. The tombs are not as colorful and elaborate as Buddhist and Daoist structures, and only three have been restored and are open to the public, however the necropolis is definitely a worthwhile stop-off as part of an excursion to the Great Wall *(see pp26–7)*.

Eastern Qing Tombs

The remoteness of the Eastern Qing Tombs, over the border in Hebei province, makes them far less popular than their Ming counterparts, despite the fact that the setting is even more splendid. In fact, the Eastern Qing Tombs make up the largest and most complete imperial cemetery in China, built on a scale as grand as the Forbidden City. Of the many tombs here, only five are the burial places of Qing emperors, but there are also 14 empresses, and 136 imperial consorts. Notable are the tomb of the Qianlong Emperor, with an incredible tomb chamber adorned with Buddhist carvings, and the lavish tomb of the devious Empress Cixi *(see p23)*. ◎ *77 miles (125 km) E of Beijing, Zuahua County, Hebei Province • May–Oct 8am–5:30pm daily; Nov–Apr 9am–4:30pm daily*

Spirit Tower, Ming Tombs

> *Most sights outside of Beijing have little to offer in the way of dining options, so it's wise to pack your own food*

Western Qing Tombs

If few tourists ever visit the Eastern Qing Tombs, fewer still make it out here to their equally distant western counterparts. Again, this is another vast burial complex comprising over 70 tombs in all, set in spectacular surroundings. Tombs include those of the emperors Daoguang, Guangxu, Jiaqing, and Yongzheng (r. 1723–35). It was the latter who founded this particular necropolis, perhaps because he could not bear to be buried beside his father, whose will he had thwarted when he seized the throne from his brother, the nominated heir. Also here, in a nearby commercial cemetery, are the remains of Pu Yi, the last emperor of China (see p9). Ⓢ 68 miles (110 km) SW of Beijing, Yixian County, Hebei Province • May–Oct 8am–5:30pm daily; Nov–Apr 9am–4:30pm daily

Chuandixia

Situated on a steep mountainside, Chuandixia is a crumbling but still picturesque hamlet of courtyard houses (siheyuan), most dating from the Ming and Qing dynasties. An entry ticket allows access to the entire village, all of which can be explored in a few hours. The population consists of about 70 people spread over a handful of families. Accommodation with one of the families can be provided for those wanting an experience of rural hospitality. Ⓢ Near Zhaitang town, 56 miles (90 km) W of Beijing • Subway to Pingguo Yuan (1 hr), then taxi

Tanzhe Temple

This enormous temple dates back to the 3rd century AD, when it was known as Jiafu Si. It was later renamed for the adjacent mountain, Tanzhe Shan. It has a splendid mountainside setting, and its halls rise up the steep incline. The temple is especially famous for its ancient trees. Ⓢ 28 miles (45 km) W of Beijing • 6086 2505 • Subway to Pingguo Yuan (1 hr), then bus 931 or tourist bus 7 • 8am–5pm daily

Stupa Forest Temple

Near the parking lot for the Tanzhe Temple is this even more fascinating temple, notab

Chuandixia village

r its marvelous collection
brick stupas hidden among
e foliage. Each stupa was
nstructed in memory of a
nowned monk. The towering
difices were built in a variety
designs, and the earliest
nong them dates from the
n dynasty (1115–1234).
28 miles (45 km) W of Beijing • 6086
05 • Subway to Pingguo Yuan (1 hr),
en bus 931 or tourist bus 7 • 8am–
m daily

Marco Polo Bridge
Straddling the Yongding River
ear Wanping town, the 876-ft
67-m) marble bridge was first
uilt during the Jin dynasty in
89 but was destroyed by a
ood. The current structure dates
1698. The bridge acquired its
me when legendary voyager
arco Polo described it in his
mous treatise *The Travels*. The
alustrades along the length
the bridge are decorated by
ore than 400 stone lions, each
ne slightly different from all
e others. On July 7, 1937, the
apanese Imperial Army and
ationalist Chinese soldiers
xchanged fire at the bridge, an
cident that led to the Japanese
ccupation of Beijing and war.
10 miles (16 km) SW of Beijing • Bus
9 from Beijing's Lianhuachi bus station
7am–7pm daily

Peking Man Site
In the 1920s, archeologists
moved from a cave at
oukoudian some 40-odd
ssilized bones and primitive
plements, which they
entified as the prehistoric
mains of Peking Man. It was
ought that this exciting
scovery provided the much
ught-after link between
eanderthals and modern
mans. Designated a UNESCO

Stupa Forest Temple

World Heritage site, the area
is geared toward specialists,
although the small museum has
an interesting collection of tools,
and bone fragments. Peking Man
himself is not here – his remains
mysteriously disappeared during
World War II. *30 miles (48 km) SW
of Beijing • Bus 917 from Beijing's
Tianqiao station to Fangshan, then taxi
• 8:30am–4:30pm daily*

Shidu
Shidu offers a fabulous
escape from the commotion of
urban Beijing and a chance to
enjoy some stunning natural
scenery. Before the new road
and bridges were built, travelers
had to cross the Juma River ten
times as they journeyed through
the gorge between Shidu and
nearby Zhangfang village, hence
the name Shidu, which means
"Ten Crossings." Pleasant
walking trails wind along the
riverbank between impressive
gorges and limestone
formations. *62 miles (100 km) SW
of Beijing • Train daily from Beijing's
Yongding Men station to Shidu*

STREETSMART

BEIJING'S TOP 10

Above left to right **Spring, summer, fall, and winter in Beijing**

Planning Your Visit

1 When to Go
Spring and fall are the best times to visit. Summer is unbearably hot, while winter is fiercely cold and gloomy. Planning your trip to coincide with one of the major festival periods *(see pp34–5)* can lead to a colorful trip, although tourist sights will be swamped.

2 Length of Stay
You need at least four full days to take in the highlights (which would include the Forbidden City, Temple of Heaven, Summer Palace, and Great Wall). This would make for an exhausting schedule and you'd still miss out on plenty. Six or seven days would allow you to experience the best of Beijing at a more comfortable pace.

3 What to Bring
November through March you need a warm jacket, gloves, sweater, thermal leggings, sturdy footwear, and lip balm. In summer, you need only loose-fitting shirts or T-shirts and thin trousers. Also bring a raincoat (it can pour down in July and August), sun hat, and reading material, as English-language books aren't easy to come by.

4 Visas and Passports
A passport, valid for at least six months, and a visa are necessary to enter China. Its embassies and consulates issue a standard single-entry, 30-day visa, although longer-stay multiple-entry visas can also be obtained.

5 Immunizations
Ensure that all of your routine vaccinations, such as tetanus, polio, and diphtheria, are up to date. It is advisable also to get vaccinated against Hepatitis A and B, typhoid, meningococcal meningitis, and cholera. Visitors traveling from yellow fever hotspots must provide proof of vaccination against the disease.

6 Customs
Visitors to China are entitled to a duty-free allowance of 2 liters of wine or spirits and 400 cigarettes. Foreign currency exceeding US$5,000, or its equivalent, must be declared. It is not advisable to take in politically controversial literature, especially if it is written in Chinese.

7 Language
The official language of China is Putonghua, known outside China as Mandarin. Putonghua is the native language of the north, but it is used across the country for communication between speakers of several other Chinese languages. English is not widely spoken outside of hotels.

8 Health Matters
Take out medical insurance before you travel. Beijing has priva hospitals, but they are expensive. Pharmacies *(yaodian)*, identified by green crosses, are plentiful. They stock bo Western and Chinese medicine, and can trea you for minor ailments.

9 Security
Beijing is generally safe, and foreign visito are unlikely to be the victims of crime, apart from petty theft, and occasional scams. Friendly Chinese who suggest a chat over tea may be in cahoots with bar or café and looking land you with a pumpe up bill. Hotels are reliab secure, but manageme don't accept responsibi should anything vanish. Be discreet when takin out your wallet and tak particular care of bags, purses, and wallets at crowded tourist sites.

10 Local Prices
In general prices are cheap. Admission t most sights (the likes c the Forbidden City and Great Wall excepted) is less than a dollar. If yo avoid hotel restaurants then you can eat well f under $10 a head. Taxis are cheap enough to be a viable way of getting around; expect to pay t equivalent of a dollar o two for most short trip around town.

ove **Local newspapers and magazines**

10 Sources of Information

1 Tourist Information

hina has yet to realize e value of professional urist information nters. Those in Beijing e underfunded and orly staffed. The ate-approved China ternational Travel rvice (CITS), originally t up to cater to the eds of foreign visitors, day functions as any her local operator, fering nothing more an tours, tickets, and nted cars.

2 Websites

There are many cellent sites offering ormation on Beijing, d China in general. e best starting point is ww.beijingpage.com, hich is a gateway to any other useful sites. e official Beijing urism Administration e (www.bjta.gov.cn) is od for what's going on the city.

3 Foreign Newspapers and agazines

reign press is hard come by, with just a all selection available some of the larger tels. You can usually t *Time*, *Newsweek*, e *International Herald bune*, and *Asian Wall reet Journal* – providing ne of them carry icles critical of China, which case that rticular edition will t be on the shelves.

4 Local Newspapers and Magazines

The government's English-language mouthpiece is the woeful *China Daily*. More worthwhile are the many English-language magazines aimed at expats and distributed free around the city's bars and restaurants; these include *Beijing Talk*, *City Weekend*, and *that's Beijing*, all of which are published monthly.

5 English-Language TV and Radio

The state-run Chinese Central Television (CCTV) has CCTV9 as its flagship English-language station. Cable and satellite television with BBC and CNN is available in top-end hotels. The Chinese radio network, has only a few local English-language programs.

6 Guides and Maps

There are some very good maps available of Beijing but you won't find them in China. Pick them up at home before you travel. Given the amount of changes taking place, it's vital that you buy the most recent map you can find. Anything more than just two or three years old will be of little use.

7 Business Information

The first place to start is the trade section of your own embassy in Beijing. Otherwise there are several trade promotion organizations including the American Chamber of Commerce, the British Chamber of Commerce, and the China Council for the Promotion of International Trade.

8 Olympic Games

Visit www.beijing 2008.com for news and information concerning the upcoming games.

9 Background Reading: Non-fiction

Mr China by Tim Clissold is a terrific account of how to lose millions of dollars doing business with Beijing. *Mao* is Jung Chang's lacerating biography of the Great Leader, banned in China. *Foreign Babes in Beijing* by Rachel DeWoskin is the memoir of a sexually liberated American girl gatecrashing modern Chinese society.

10 Background Reading: Fiction

Balzac and the Little Chinese Seamstress by Dai Sijie is a beautiful novella tracking the lives of two childhood friends enduring Mao's Cultural Revolution. *Wild Swans* by Jung Chang is the gripping story of three generations of women living though 20th-century China. *Big Breasts and Wide Hips* is the latest saga by Mo Yan, an epic of Chinese history, politics, hunger, religion, love, and sex.

Left **By biycle** Center **By taxi** Right **By bus**

⑩ Getting Around

Beijing Airport
On arrival visitors are given up to three forms to complete: health, immigration, and customs, all submitted to officials between the plane and the arrivals hall. Here there are ATMs, foreign exchange counters, public telephones, left-luggage services, over-priced restaurants, and a limited number of shops.

From the Airport into Town
There are plans to extend the subway out to the airport but for the moment taking a taxi is the easiest option. Taxis wait for passengers at a marshaled rank outside the arrivals hall. If you have a hotel booked, check whether it offers a courtesy airport pick-up.

Subway
The subway is a swift way to get around and to avoid Beijing's legendarily stationary traffic. The system is easy to use and fares are extremely cheap. Buy tickets at the booths near the station entrances.

Buses
The city bus network is extensive and cheap. Most trips within the city center require a flat flare, which is clearly posted on the side of the bus; typically ¥1 or ¥2. Air-conditioned services are usually a little more expensive. However, near-perpetual traffic jams mean journeys can often be unnecessarily lengthy. In addition, buses are almost always over-crowded and destinations are given in Chinese only.

Taxis
Taxis are found in large numbers and can be hailed easily in the street. Make sure the driver uses the meter, which they usually only start once the journey is actually under way – so wait a moment, then say, "Dabiao" (meter), if necessary. Few taxi drivers speak English, so have your destination written down in Chinese by your hotel staff. Fares per kilometer (half mile) are clearly posted on the side of the car; these are usually ¥1.60 or ¥2.

Cycling
Hiring a bicycle can be a great way to explore. Bike lanes are common and roadside repair stalls are every-where. Beijing is flat and very cyclable, but if you are not used to cycling in heavy traffic, it can be an intimidating experience. Handy bike stands are found all over and have an attendant to watch the bikes for a modest fee.

Rickshaws
Bicycle rickshaws, once common in Beijing, are now relegated to the lakeside area of Hou Hai, north of the Forbidden City, where they offer tours of the old *hutong* (alleys) to tourists. There are also rickshaws in the neighborhood of Ri Tan Park east of the center, which are used by locals to ferry them around after shopping at the area's various markets.

Walking
Beijing is not a great city for walking. Most streets are inhumanely wide and traffic pollution can be choking. The few exceptions include the Hou Hai area and the embassy districts of Ri Tan Park and Sanlitun. Parks such as Bei Hai, Chaoyang, Di Tan, and the Temple of Heaven Park, are also excellent places for wandering.

Tours
Most hotels in Beijing organize tours around the major city sights, as well as out of town to the Ming Tombs and Great Wall. Even if you are not staying at the hotel in question, they are usually only too happy to sign you up for an excursion.

Waterways
During the summer months tour boats ply the city's ancient canal system. From 10am to 4pm there are sailings the hour from Yuyuan Tan Park, near the Millennium Monument *(see p91)*, and from the Beijing Exhibition Hall *(see p92)*, out to the Summer Palace.

t Automated tellers **Center** Sidewalk card telephones **Right** Chinese *renminbi*

10 Banking and Communications

Currency
China's currency is
led *yuan*, also written
renminbi and referred
in spoken language as
ai. One *yuan* divides
o 10 *jiao*. The most
mmon coins include
yuan, and 5 and 1 *jiao*.
ls in circulation are 1,
and 5 *jiao*, and 1, 2, 5,
, 20, 50, and 100 *yuan*.

Changing Money
You can exchange
rrency at major banks
d international airports.
ost decent hotels will
ange money, but for
ests only. Exchange
es are decided
ntrally. Convert any
-over *renminbi* back
fore you leave,
hough usually only
change counters at
ports and ports will do
s. You must present
cent exchange or ATM
ceipts for double the
ount you want to re-
change.

Automated Tellers
The Automated
lers (ATMs) that
cept foreign cards
principally those
onging to the Bank
China. Occasionally (at
jing Capital Airport for
tance) other Chinese
nk ATMs work too, but
presence of familiar
os on the screen does
guarantee that
eign cards will work.
ere are many usable
Ms in banks, shopping
lls, and hotels around
city center.

Credit Cards
Credit cards are
widely accepted in
upscale restaurants
and top-end hotels, and
in large tourist shops,
but always check before
attempting to make
a purchase that your
foreign card is accepted.
The commonly accepted
cards are MasterCard,
Visa, JCB, Diners Club,
and American Express.

Traveler's Checks
Some hotel foreign
exchange counters will
no longer exchange
checks, and will send you
to the Bank of China. All
popular foreign brands
are accepted, but
occasionally cashiers
nervous of responsibility
will reject those that look
unfamiliar. Keep the
proof of purchase slips
and a record of the serial
numbers in case of loss
or theft.

Post
It takes as little as
four days to send airmail
and postcards overseas.
Visitors can send mail by
standard or registered
post, while EMS
(Express Mail Service)
is a reliable way to send
packages and documents
abroad and within the
country. Most post
offices are open seven
days a week.

Telephones
International and
long-distance phone calls
can be made from most

hotels and card
telephones. It is usually
necessary to ask
receptionists or operators
to place the calls. In
cheaper hotels you may
be asked to first pay a
deposit. Most public
phones require an IC
(integrated circuit) card,
sold in shops and kiosks
wherever the letters "IC"
are seen.

Calling Beijing
To call China from
abroad, dial your
international access
code, China's country
code 86, then 10 for
Beijing, followed by the
local number.

Mobiles
Visitors with mobile
phones from almost
anywhere except North
America and Japan can
use the Chinese system
(Americans can only use
the Chinese system if
they have an unlocked
tri- or quad-band phone).
Just buy a local pre-paid
SIM card from any phone
shop. If you do not have
a phone compatible with
the Chinese system, the
cheapest option is to buy
one, not rent.

Internet Cafés
Personal computer
ownership is limited in
China, so internet cafés
(wangba) are common.
You can also get online
at many China Telecom
offices. Many foreign
media sites are blocked
by the government.

Left **Young Beijingers on Wangfujing** Right **Monk at the Lama Temple**

🔟 Etiquette

1 Greeting People
Shaking hands is commonplace and certainly considered the norm with foreign visitors. The usual Chinese greeting is "Ni hao," which means "How are you?" or "Nimen hao" in its plural form, to which you reply "Ni hao" or "Nimen hao."

2 Personal Questions
Although unfailingly polite, Chinese people will not blanch at asking you how much you earn, how old you are, or whether you are married. Such questions are seen as nothing more than taking a friendly interest in a new acquaintance.

3 Exchanging Business Cards
When proffering business cards, the Chinese do so using the fingertips of both hands, and receive cards in the same manner. For businessmen a good supply of cards is essential, preferably with English on one side and Chinese on the reverse.

4 Face
Although reserved in manner and expression, the Chinese also harbor strong feelings of personal pride and respect. The maintenance of pride and avoidance of shame is a concept known as "face." Loss of face creates great discomfort and major

embarrassment for Chinese, so although you may occasionally become frustrated by delays or the incompetence of hotel staff, it is never a good idea to embarrass anybody in public.

5 Places of Worship
Buddhist, Daoist, and Confucian temples are relaxed about visitors wandering about, but you should be considerate toward worshipers and the resident monks, and refrain from sticking cameras in their faces. You need to dress more respectfully for mosques – avoid wearing shorts or short skirts, and cover your upper arms.

6 Staring
The Chinese habit of staring can be a little annoying. This sort of behavior is normally encountered in smaller towns and rural areas, but you also come across it in Beijing, since the city attracts a lot of migrant workers and peasant tourists. However, the intent is never hostile.

7 Tipping
The Chinese do not tip. so neither should you, and that goes for guides, bell boys, taxi drivers, and anyone else. In China the price you agree for the service is the one you pay, although some restaurants in larger hotels now

routinely add a service charge. Away from hotel and tourist areas waitresses will pursue you down the street to return the change they think you've forgotten.

8 Begging
China's imbalanced economic progress and huge population of rural poor have resulted in large numbers of beggars, especially in Beijing and other big cities. Foreign visitors are associated with wealth and naturally attract lot of attention, and group of children are often set by their parents to extract money. The best strategy is to ignore them and walk away.

9 Political Discussion
Avoid political discussion altogether. Most Chinese are very uncomfortable hearing criticism of the leadership or nation. At the same time, they are quite happy to have a go at other countries, often to the point where you might feel provoked enough to respond. Don't. Far better to just change the subject.

10 Chinese Names
The Chinese will usually state their last name first, followed by the given name. For example, Zhang Yimou in Chinese would be Mr. Yimou Zhang using the Western style.

ove **Rush hour**

10 Things to Avoid

Students of English

ople on the street
I sometimes strike
conversation in order,
they will tell you, to
actice their English.
wever, caution is
cessary as increasingly
ese approaches are
d-ins to scams. These
called "language
dents" will often
ggest entering a
arby café or bar at
ich you will naturally
er to buy them a drink.
e students take
nerous advantage of
ur offer and then
part leaving you with
wildly inflated bill for
ousands of *renminbi*.
course, the bar owner
n on the deal.

Queuing

The Chinese don't
queues. They prefer to
sh and shove. Anyone
o politely waits their
n at the ticket office is
ely to be stood there
day.

Taking Offense at Spitting

nough there is always
rack-down in the run-
to major international
ents, such as the 2008
ympics, and despite
e best attempts of
olic educators, spitting
mains a fact of Chinese
on the streets, buses
d trains. It is not just
old man thing either;
s not uncommon to
serve a pretty young
man break off mid-

conversation to loudly
expel a gob of saliva.

4 Rush Hour

Beijing's traffic is
horrendous and if you
aren't careful you could
spend half your visit sat
in a taxi, gridlocked in a
sea of other vehicles.
Rush hour seems to last
nearly all day, but the
roads are noticeably
worse on week days
before 10am and
between around 5pm
and 8pm. You should
avoid traveling at these
times if at all possible.

5 Art Students

Around Wangfujing
Dajie, Liulichang, Tian'an
Men Square and the
Forbidden City, be wary
of "art students" who in
the guise of fund-raising
will pressure you to visit
an exhibition where you
can buy amateur and
hugely overpriced art.

6 Guides

At many of Beijing's
sights, but particularly at
the Forbidden Palace and
Temple of Heaven, so-
called guides wait around
the ticket offices to offer
their services. Decline.
They usually know little
more than the bare
facts, which are often
recited with a dubious
propagandist slant.

7 Visiting Sights on National Holidays

The biggest tourists in
China are the Chinese
themselves. On public

holidays out-of-towners
swarm into Beijing for
a spot of sightseeing. It
becomes impossible to
move in the Forbidden
City, Temple of Heaven,
or in any of the parks.

8 Sweet and Sour Chicken

China's is one of the
world's great cuisines.
Chinese food is
astonishing in its variety,
and there is nowhere
better to experience this
than Beijing. The city
boasts restaurants
specializing in most, if
not all, the country's
many regional cuisines.
Ordering the few
Cantonese-originating
dishes that have come
to represent Chinese
cooking to the rest of the
world would really be a
wasted opportunity.

9 Public Toilets

In general, public
toilets are hole-in-the-
ground types and are
usually extremely
malodorous. You will
need to bring your own
tissue paper as it is
seldom available. Take
advantage of the facilities
in top-end hotels and
restaurants.

10 Taking a Taxi without the Right Change

Beijing taxi drivers hardly
ever seem to carry any
change, so make sure
you always have a good
stash of ¥5, ¥10, and ¥20
notes to hand.

Left **Exotic food at the Night Market** Right **Western-style restaurant**

Dining in Beijing

Restaurant areas
Beijing boasts literally thousands, if not tens of thousands, of restaurants. The best areas to wander in order to see what's on offer are around Hou Hai (see pp20–21) and along Ghost Street (see p87) for Chinese cuisine. For the widest choice of international restaurants, try the streets on the south side of Ri Tan Park (see p85) and those on the north and west sides of the Workers' Stadium (see p86) in the diplomatic and entertainment district of Sanlitun.

Strange foods
Should you so wish then, yes, you can find the likes of dog, snake, sea slug, scorpions, and penises from a variety of animals on the menus of Beijing restaurants. However, none of these are particularly common dishes and you are unlikely to find them on the table in front of you without specifically seeking them out.

Chinese menus
Many restaurants have menus in Chinese only. In which case, it is perfectly acceptable to look around at what people on other tables are eating and just point to what you fancy.

International cuisine
Beijing is a modern, international city and many of its international restaurants are truly world class, notably those described on pages 60–61. If you should tire of Chinese cuisine then without too much trouble you can find restaurants here that will do a great burger or an authentic spaghetti bolognaise.

Eating with chopsticks
Chinese restaurants set their tables with chopsticks, not knives and forks. If you have never eaten with chopsticks before then it's wise to get in a little practice before your visit to Beijing, otherwise you could find yourself on an unexpected crash diet.

Décor
Many Beijing restaurants appear very basic, even scruffy, with Formica tables, cheap furnishings, and plastic tableware. Chinese tend not to care about things like the aesthetics, the ambience, and the service. Instead what they care about is the quality of the food. Little else matters.

Street food
Chinese street food is plentiful, varied, and usually delicious (see p57). The best place to try it is at one of the two street-food markets off Wangfujing Dajie (see p71). There are also lots of street-food vendors in the Hou Hai area (see pp20–21).

Meal times
The Chinese tend to eat early. Lunch can be served as early as 11am and many restaurants will stop serving at 2pm. Dinner typically starts at around 5pm, with many restaurant kitchens closed by 9:30pm.

Late-night eating
Many of the hotel restaurants stay open late, as do a cluster of places around the west gate of the Workers' Stadium, notably the excellent Bellagio (see p58). A lot of bars serve decent food until the early hours, including The Tree (see p63), while most of the restaurants along Ghost Street (see p87) remain open 24 hours daily.

Dining with Chinese
As a guest of Chinese hosts it is polite to sample all of the dishes on the table, although you should leave something on the plate at the end of the meal. A clean plate indicates you are still hungry. Drinking is an important part of Chinese entertaining, but do not pour your own drink – it shows a lack of protocol. The most common expression for toasting is "Gan bei", meaning "dry the glass" or "bottoms up."

Left **Dazhalan street market** Right **Low-cost clothing at the Silk Market**

10 Shopping Tips

Opening hours
Most shops and markets are open from around 9am daily and do not close until around 8pm, or later.

Haggling
The Chinese haggle even in shops with fixed prices and it pays for you to do the same. Haggling in markets is essential – traders will start by quoting you a price that can be 10 times or more beyond what is fair. Your first offer must always be a fraction of what they ask. For example, a trader who starts by demanding ¥150 for a jacket at the Silk Market will probably be prepared to let it go for as little as ¥30; offer ¥10 and then walk away, and listen as the price plummets.

Credit cards
Credit cards are only accepted at branches of international stores and luxury boutiques, and department stores. Always check just which cards are accepted and carry enough cash to cover in case your plastic is rejected.

Fakes
Beijing is awash with fakes, from counterfeit Rolex watches to careful copies of North Face jackets. Some of these are extremely well done, with counterfeiters even going so far as to replicate the internal workings of

watches. Of course, it is all illegal. The piracy is likely to be stamped out, or at least sent underground, by the time the 2008 Olympic Games come around. Until then, a shopping session at the Silk Market *(see p88)* remains high on most tourists' list.

Bargains
Counterfeit goods and fakes aside, there are few real bargains to be had in Beijing. No matter how good your haggling skills, no market trader ever sells at a loss, or even at anything like cost price (despite what they tell you). The antiques are anything but old and even the Mao memorabilia is made specifically for the tourist trade. The simple rule is, buy something because you like it, not because you have been told that it is worth a great deal.

DVDs and CDs
As well as fake clothing, Beijing is awash with pirate DVDs and CDs, sold openly from specialist stores. Movies appear on disc even before they've been premiered. Some of the less recent releases are highly professional with all the added extras. However, some disks just won't play at all. It's a bit of a gamble and, again, the flow of product is likely to dry up in the run up to the 2008 Olympics.

Tailoring
If you have the time and the inclination, one of the most satisfying shopping experiences is to buy some cloth and have a local tailor make up clothes to your own design or specifications. Present them with an example and they can make exact copies of your favorite shirts or trousers. They can even work from pictures in a magazine. Yaxiu Market *(see p88)* in Sanlitun has the greatest number of tailors, plus plenty of stalls selling cloth.

Refunds
Make sure that you really want what you're buying because there is no such thing as a refund in China.

Shopping areas
Beijing's main shopping street is Wangfujing Dajie *(see p68)*. Other good places include the Dazhalan and Liulichang *(see p73)* areas south of Tian'an Men Square, and on and off Sanlitun Bei Lu.

Electronics
Don't mix up Beijing with Hong Kong: there are no bargain electronics here. Most hardware is imported and so costs significantly more than in your home country. You can get cheap Chinese-made equivalents but these are unreliable and there is no warranty.

Left **Peninsula Palace Hotel** Right **Commune at the Great Wall**

Accommodation Tips

Area options
Distances in Beijing are vast and roads are perpetually choked with traffic, so if you don't want to spend half your visit sat in the back of a succession of taxis, be careful when choosing your hotel. Unless business requires you to be elsewhere, then aim to stay as close to the Forbidden City as possible. In a choice of east side versus west, favor the former, for its better restaurants and shopping.

Hotel standards
For international standards of comfort and service, stick to five-star hotels managed by familiar Western chains, or the Singapore- and Hong Kong-based luxury companies. Chinese-run operations do their best to emulate foreign hotels but typically the only way in which they come close is in the pricing.

Star system
The Chinese star system of grading hotels is meaningless, since no star has ever lost once it has been given, despite sometimes dramatic deterioration.

Something different
Other than a couple of pricey options (Red Capital Residence and the Commune at the Wall), the boutique hotel has yet to catch on in China. However, what Beijing does have is lots of courtyard hotels. These are conversions of traditional *siheyuan* (courtyard houses) in old *hutong* (alley) areas of the city. These vary in price and degree of comforts from budget to expensive luxury options.

Booking and bargaining
For most foreign-run hotels the best price will be found on the hotel's own website. However, websites for Chinese hotels will always quote a wildly inflated rack rate. In China, the real price of a hotel room is what the customer is willing to pay. Locals will always ask for a discount and you should too – you can do this by email if you are booking in advance from overseas.

Payment
Outside of the major international hotels you may find that only Chinese versions of well-known credit cards are accepted, so make a point of asking when you check in. Hotel foreign exchange facilities are becoming less reliable and holders of traveler's checks in particular, may be sent to a bank. In more modest hotels always be prepared to settle your bill in *renminbi*. Also, be aware that it is normal for most Chinese-run hotels to a for payment of your roc in advance.

Hidden extras
Service charges of between five and fiftee percent are frequently added to the final bill, so clarify this at the start. Minibar contents are as overpriced in China as they are anywhere else, but international telephone calls made from your room are subject to on a modest surcharge.

Seasonal deman
The busiest travel periods are during the week-long national holidays that occur around May 1 and October 1, and during the Chinese New Year *(see p34)*. If you are planning to be in China at any of these times then you should make any hotel (and domesti travel) reservations we in advance.

Traveling with kids
Most hotels allow und 12s to stay with their parents free of charge. Most will also add an extra bed for an older child for a nominal (and negotiable) fee.

Tipping
Traditionally there i no tipping in China and hotel staff may even tr to return money that is left for them.

Price Categories

For a standard, double room per night (with breakfast if included), taxes and extra charges.

¥	under ¥200
¥¥	¥200–¥400
¥¥¥	¥400–¥800
¥¥¥¥	¥800–¥1400
¥¥¥¥¥	over ¥1400

ve Grand Hyatt Beijing

Luxury and Boutique Hotels

China World Hotel
The most luxurious
el in Beijing, and often
choice of visiting
ds of state. It's in
heart of the Central
siness District (CBD),
ve a swish shopping
l and it has arguably
best restaurant in
n in Aria (see p60).
Jianguo Men Wai Dajie
ap H4 • 6505 2266 •
way: Guomao • ¥¥¥¥¥
ww.shangri-la.com

**Commune at
the Great Wall**
ven modern villas by
Asian architects dot
een valley within
nt of the Great Wall.
ilities include DVD
ers, an indoor pool,
a private cinema.
naged by Kempinski.
Badaling, 30 miles
km) NW of Beijing
18 1888 • ¥¥¥¥¥ •
w.commune.com.cn

**Grand Hyatt
Beijing**
ve the Oriental Plaza
l on Wangfujing, no
er luxury hotel is better
ted; few are as well
ipped. Restaurants
e are among the city's
st and the pool is a
ck-out. ℘ 1 Dong
ng'an Jie • Map N5
18 1234 • Subway:
ngfujing • ¥¥¥¥¥ •
w.beijing.grand.hyatt.

Kerry Center Hotel
The youngest of
ngri-La's Beijing
ple combines the

group's high service
standards with bright,
modern room design. The
Kerry is also home to the
city's hottest cocktail bar
and extensive health
facilities. ℘ 1 Guanghua
Lu • Map H4 • 6561 8833
• Subway: Guomao • ¥¥¥¥¥
• www.shangri-la.com

**5 Peninsula Palace
Hotel**
Luxurious and recently
renovated rooms have
large plasma TVs; marble
bathrooms also have a
small screen. Two terrific
restaurants (Huang Ting
and Jing), a luxury mall,
excellent service, and a
central location, make
this one of the city's best
choices. ℘ 8 Jinyu Hutong
• Map N4 • 8516 2888
• Subway: Dengshikou •
¥¥¥¥¥ • www.peninsula.
com

**6 Red Capital
Residence**
Beijing's quirkiest hotel
has just five rooms, each
furnished with period
antiques and decorated
according to a different
theme. You can choose
from the "Chairman's
Suite" or one of the
"Concubines' Private
Courtyards". ℘ 66 Dong
Si Liutiao • Map F2 • 8403
5308 • Subway: Dong Si
Shi Tiao • ¥¥¥¥¥ • www.
redcapitalclub.com.cn

7 Shangri-La Beijing
Recently renovated to
a high standard, and with
the addition of a brand
new tower and excellent

restaurants and bars.
One drawback is that
the hotel is out in the
far west of the city, near
the Summer Palace.
℘ 29 Zizhu Yuan Lu • 6841
2211 • ¥¥¥¥¥ • www.
shangri-la.com

8 St. Regis Beijing
Small but beautifully
decorated rooms with
free access to an on-call
butler. There are excellent
restaurants, as well as an
exclusive health club and
outdoor putting green.
℘ 21 Jianguo Men Wai
Dajie • Map G4 • 6460
6688 • ¥¥¥¥¥ • www.
stregis.com/beijing

9 The Ascott Beijing
Acclaimed top-end
living for international
executives in the heart of
the CBD, also providing
1–3 bedroom apartments.
Service is exceptional
and apartments are
elegantly furnished and
fully equipped. ℘ 108B
Jianguo Lu • Map H4
• 6567 8100 • Subway:
Guomao • ¥¥¥¥¥ • www.
theascottbeijing.com

10 Beijing Hotel
Beijing's oldest hotel
reopened in summer
2006 after a massive refit
as part of the famed
Raffles group. Excellent
location at the bottom of
Wangfujing, a short walk
from Tian'an Men Square.
℘ 33 Dong Chang'an Jie •
Map M5 • 6513 7766 •
Subway: Wangfujing •
¥¥¥¥¥ • www.chinabeijing
hotel.com.cn

*Unless otherwise stated, all hotels listed above accept credit
cards, have en-suite bathrooms, and air-conditioning*

Left **Kempinski Hotel** Right **Wangfujing Grand**

Business and High-end Hotels

Beijing Hilton
A recent refurb has transformed the Hilton into a stylish hotel with large rooms sporting designer flourishes and huge bathrooms. Good value option close to the embassies, shopping, and nightlife centers of Nuren Jie and Sanlitun. ⊗ 1 Dong Fang Lu • Map H1 • 5865 5000 • ¥¥¥¥ • www.beijing.hilton.com

Crowne Plaza
Comfortable rooms with tasteful decoration give onto a nine-story atrium. Reasonable value, and within walking distance of Wangfujing and the Forbidden City. ⊗ 48 Wangfujing Dajie • Map N3 • 6513 3388 • Subway: Wangfujing • ¥¥¥¥ • www.crowneplaza.beijing.ichotelsgroup.com

Park Plaza Hotel
The stylish new Park Plaza is a peaceful oasis in a fast developing precinct. Rooms feature designer touches and the hotel is convenient for Wangfujing Dajie and the Forbidden City. ⊗ 97 Jinbao Jie • Map N3 • 8522 1999 • Subway: Wangfujing • ¥¥¥¥ • www.parkplaza.com/beijingcn

Renaissance Hotel
Four-star business hotel close by the International Exhibition Center, also providing access to myriad dining and shopping options on Xiaoyun Lu and the adjacent Nuren Jie. Rooms are large in size, luxurious but subtle. ⊗ 36 Xiaoyun Lu • 6468 9999 • ¥¥¥¥ • www.marriott.com

Howard Johnson Paragon
Comfortable and close to Beijing Railway Station, and just a short taxi ride to Wangfujing and Tian'an Men Square. Rooms, though not large, are recently renovated, and international standards ensure a quality of service superior to that of most other nearby hotels. ⊗ 18A Jianguo Men Nei Dajie • Map F4 • 6526 6688 • Subway: Beijing Zhan • ¥¥¥¥ • www.hojochina.com

Traders Hotel Beijing
In the heart of the CBD, and offering every possible business facility, plus plenty of comforts, including an excellent Southeast Asian buffet. Next to the China World Shopping Mall and its subway station. ⊗ 1 Jianguo Men Wai Dajie • Map H4 • 6505 2277 • Subway: Guomao • ¥¥¥¥ • www.shangri-la.com

Great Wall Sheraton
Although one of the biggest hotels in Beijing, rooms are surprisingly small. Still, service is pleasant, and the Canton restaurant on the 21st floor gets good reviews. ⊗ 10 Dong San Huan Be Lu • Map H1 • 6590 556 • ¥¥¥¥ • www.sheraton.com/beijingcn

Hotel New Otani Chang Fu Gong
Targeted at high-end business travelers, this Japanese-run hotel is convenient to the CBD and offers several wor while restaurants and bars. Rooms are small but feature tasteful decoration. ⊗ 26 Jiang Men Wai Dajie • Map G • 5877 5555 • Subway: Jianguo Men • ¥¥¥¥ • www.newotani.co.jp

Kempinski Hote
Near the new Nure Jie embassy district, t Kempinski offers supe service and access to Western conveniences the attached Lufthansa Center, including bars, restaurants, and high-c shopping. ⊗ 50 Liangn Qiao Lu • Map H1 • 646 3388 • ¥¥¥¥¥ • www.kempinski-beijing.com

Wangfujing Gra
Good value in one of Beijing's priciest an most central hotel districts, with views o the Forbidden City fro the west-facing rooms There's adequate serv thanks to Hong Kong management and all new fixtures thanks to a recent renovation. ⊗ 57 Wangfujing Dajie • M N4 • 6522 1188 • Subw Wangfujing • ¥¥¥¥¥ • www.wangfujinghotel.c

Unless otherwise stated, all hotels listed above accept credit cards, have en-suite bathrooms, and air-conditioning

Price Categories

For a standard, double room per night (with breakfast if included), taxes and extra charges.

¥	under ¥200
¥¥	¥200–¥400
¥¥¥	¥400–¥800
¥¥¥¥	¥800–¥1400
¥¥¥¥¥	over ¥1400

...ve Red House Hotel

Mid-range Hotels

Fang Yuan Hotel
Two blocks north of famed Night Market, location is hard to ...t. It's a fairly modest ...ce but looking quite ...uce after a 2005 refit. ...ff are well used to ...ling with foreigners ...there's a travel ...isory service, booking ...ter, bicycle rental, and ...ernet. ◎ 36 Dengshikou ... • Map M3 • 6525 6331 ...ubway: Dengshikou • ¥¥ ...ww.cbw.com/hotel/ ...gyuan

Hade Men Hotel
Among the older ...els in Beijing, but ...ovated to a standard ...ve other Chinese-run ...ons in this range. ...oms are comfortable, ...bit gaudy, with nice ...ws from the upper ...rs. It's round the ...ner from the railway ...tion. ◎ 2A Chongwen ...n Wai Dajie • Map N6 ...711 2244 • Subway: ...ngwen Men • ¥¥ • ...w.hademenhotel.com

Red House Hotel
Dorms, hotel rooms, ...apartments with ...hens for short- or ...g-term rent. Rooms ...ure dark wooden ...rs and faux-antique ...nishings. There's a ...ular football bar on ...premises, and it's a ...rt walk to more bars ...anlitun. ◎ 10 Taiping ...ang Chunxiu Lu • Map ... • 6416 7810 • Subway: ...g Zhi Men • ¥¥ • www. ...house.com.cn

Beijing Bullion Kaiyue Hotel
Excellent, modern three-star on a narrow lane just a few minutes' walk from Wangfujing. All rooms have laptop portals, and satellite TV, and represent good value for money. ◎ 31 Ganyu Hutong, off Dong Si Nan Dajie • Map N3 • 8511 0388 • Subway: Deng Shi Kou • ¥¥¥

City Hotel Beijing
Sound mid-range option within walking distance of Sanlitun's bars, restaurants, and shops. Rooms are clean and comfortable enough, if a little dated. Staff speak some English. ◎ 4 Gongren Tiyuchang Dong Lu • Map H2 • 6500 7799 • Subway: Dong Si Shi Tiao • ¥¥¥ • www. cityhotel.com.cn

Comfort Inn & Suites
Rooms are tastefully decorated, with desks, comfortable sofas, and plush new duvets. It caters more for business people on lengthy stays, so service can be found wanting. ◎ 6 Gongren Tiyuchang Bei Lu • Map G2 • 8523 5522 • Subway: Dong Si Shi Tiao • ¥¥¥ • www.choicehotels.com

Cui Ming Zhuang Hotel
Recently renovated and cheap given the location. Rooms are simple but clean, and surprisingly large. Staff are more pleasant than is usual for a Chinese hotel. ◎ 1 Nan Heyan Dajie • Map M4 • 6513 6622 • Subway: Tian'an Men Dong • ¥¥¥ • www.cuiming zhuanghotel.com.cn

Huafeng Hotel
Blander than when it was the Grand Hôtel des Wagons-Lits, but it offers good value for money in the pleasant Legation Quarter, and is walking distance from central Tian'an Men Square and Wangfujing Street. ◎ 5 Qian Men Dong Dajie • Map M6 • 6524 7311 • Subway: Qian Men • ¥¥¥

Scitech Hotel
A good-value option for both shoppers and hedonists, the four-star Scitech abuts a large department store and popular nightclub Banana. Standard rooms are a bit on the small side but are otherwise comfortable. ◎ 22 Jianguo Men Wai Dajie • Map G4 • 6512 3388 • Subway: Jianguo Men • ¥¥¥ • www. scitechgroup.com

Qian Men Jianguo Hotel
The hotel itself isn't much to look at but rooms are decent. The Li Yun Theater, with nightly shows of Beijing Opera, is on the hotel grounds. The Temple of Heaven is a short walk away. ◎ 175 Yong'an Lu • Map D6 • 6301 6688 • Subway: Heping Men • ¥¥¥/¥¥¥¥

In Beijing's mid-range hotels credit cards are often not accepted and air-conditioning is not always standard. Check when booking

Streetsmart

Left **Bamboo Garden Hotel** Right **Lu Song Yuan Hotel**

TOP 10 Courtyard Hotels

1 Far East International Youth Hostel
Buried down in the hutongs southwest of Tian'an Men Square, this is possibly the city's cheapest old courtyard accommodations (see p117). ✆ 90 Tieshu Xie Jie • Map D5 • 5195 8561 • Subway: Heping Men • ¥ • www.hihostels.com

2 Sweet Garden Hostel
Peaceful, family-run hostel in a converted courtyard residence close to Dong Si Shi Tiao subway offers simple single, double, and 4–6 bed dorm rooms. Staff speak little English but arrange bike hire, ticket booking services, and even airport pick-up. ✆ 19 Dong Si Qi Tiao • Map G2 • 6405 1538 • Subway: Dong Si Shi Tiao • ¥

3 Friendship Guesthouse
Built in 1875 and once home to Chiang Kai Shek (you can stay in his suite) and, later, the Yugoslav Embassy. Today, it still has a bit of a Socialist feel but the courtyard setting is pleasant, and there's a Japanese restaurant on site. ✆ 7 Houyuan Ensi Hutong • Map E1 • 6403 1114 • Subway: Anding Men • ¥¥

4 Bamboo Garden Hotel
Close to the lakes, this is the oldest of Beijing's traditional hotels, with the largest and most elaborate courtyards, plus rockeries and covered pathways. ✆ 24 Xiao Shi Qiao Hutong • Map E1 • 5852 0088 • Subway: Gulou Dajie • ¥¥¥ • www.bbgh.com.cn

5 Hao Yuan Guesthouse
Smallest, most obscure, and possibly most pleasant courtyard hotel in Beijing. Rooms in the tree-shaded rear courtyard are exquisite. Walking distance to Wangfujing. ✆ 53 Shijia Hutong, Dongdan Bei Dajie • Map N3 • 6512 5557 • Subway: Dongdan • ¥¥¥ • www.haoyuanhotel.com

6 Hejing Fu Hotel
One of the largest courtyard hotels in town, Hejing Fu occupies three courtyards in total, each dotted with intricately carved statuary. Suites are luxuriously appointed with traditional trappings that reflect the house's imperial pedigree. ✆ 7 Zhangzi Dadao, Ping'an Dadao • Map N1 • 6401 7744 • Subway: Anding Men • ¥¥¥

7 Lu Song Yuan Hotel
The details are similar to those in other courtyard hotels, but here they add up to a more comfortable atmosphere. Rooms range from cheap youth hostel-style facilities right up to suites. There's also a charming teahouse a well-stocked bookshelv ✆ 22 Banchang Hutong, Kuan Jie • Map N1 • 640 0436 • Subway: Anding Men • ¥¥¥ • www.the-s road.com

8 Qomolangma Hotel
A few minutes' walk from the Drum and Be Towers and located in former Buddhist temp this courtyard hotel is full of character. Simp cosy rooms have Ming style furniture. ✆ 149 Gulou Xi Dajie • Map E1 • 6401 8822 • Subway: Gulou Dajie • ¥¥¥

9 La Suite Interdit
Exclusive, privately owned courtyard residence that include two rustic but charmin self-contained units (n for separate hire) offer a slice of imperial livin five minutes' walk fro the Forbidden City. ✆ Bei Chizi Er Tiao • Map I • Subway: Tian'an Men Dong • ¥¥¥¥¥ • suite_ interdite@yahoo.com

10 Red Capital Residence
Beijing's most uniquel louche hotel, in which those with a suitably fat wallet can live out fantasies of Old Pekin also happens to be a converted courtyard residence (see p113). ✆ 9 Dong Si Liutiao • 8 5308 • Subway: Dong S Shi Tiao • ¥¥¥¥¥ • www redcapitalclub.com.cn

116

In courtyard hotels credit cards are often not accepted and air-conditioning is not always standard. Check when booking

Price Categories

For a standard, double room per night (with breakfast if included), taxes and extra charges.

¥	under ¥200
¥¥	¥200–¥400
¥¥¥	¥400–¥800
¥¥¥¥	¥800–¥1400
¥¥¥¥¥	over ¥1400

Budget Hotels

Beijing City Youth Hostel

od value and very venient for those with y morning trains from ing Zhan. Twin rooms dorms are relatively w and clean, and there cooking facilities and 4-hour shop. ⚅ 1 ing Zhan Qian Jie • Map • 6525 8066 • Subway: ing Zhan • ¥

Leo Hostel

Excellent location th of Tian'an Men are, in among old o. Rooms range from ied dorms to doubles; ities range from cle hire to a second-d book exchange. ⚅ Guang Ju Yuan, Dazhalan • Map L6 • 6303 1595 ibway: Qian Men • ¥ ww.leohostel.com

Downtown Backpackers

od value in the heart ne of Beijing's most ant hutongs. It's also utes from the lakes, myriad restaurants bars. Offers clean ile rooms, doubles i attached bath, and bed dorms, plus bike and laundry. ⚅ 85 Luo Gu Xiang • Map 8400 2429 • Subway: ng Men • ¥

Far East International th Hostel

city's most charming hostel, with dorms private rooms in l and courtyard

settings. The area was an imperial-era red-light district and remains lively. ⚅ 90 Tieshu Xie Jie • Map K6 • 5195 8561 • Subway: Heping Men • ¥ • www.hihostels.com

5 Feiying International Youth Hostel

Among the cheapest of Beijing's HI hostels and the most convenient for transport. Private twins and dorms are pristine, and management are helpful. Facilities include a recently opened bar and restaurant. ⚅ 10 Xuanwu Men Xi Dajie • Map C4 • 6317 1116 • Subway: Changchun Jie • ¥ • www.hihostels.com

6 Saga International Youth Hostel

Featuring spotless doubles, triples, and dorm rooms, a communal kitchen and café, and a roof-top patio. Helpful English-speaking management organize ticket bookings and tours. ⚅ 9 Shijia Hutong • Map N3 • 6527 2773 • Subway: Dongdan • ¥

7 Dexinju Binguan

Chinese-managed hotel in a hutong close to Wangfujing. Staff speak little English, but rooms are bright and airy with clean bathrooms. Those on upper floors offer pleasant views. ⚅ 78 Dong Si Liu Tiao • Map N2 • 6404 2944 • Subway: Dong Si Shi Tiao • ¥

8 Xindadu Youth Hostel

One of the newest of the YHA hostels. Dorm beds (200 in total) are the only option, but rooms are pristine. Convenient for access to Beijing West Railway Station. ⚅ Chegongzhuang Dajie 21 • Map A4 • 6831 9988 ext. 185 • Subway: Chegong Zhuang • ¥¥

9 Poachers Inn

In the middle of the Sanlitun bar district, this is the hostel if you like your accommodations loud and lively. Rooms are simple and share bathrooms, but facilities are clean. Breakfast and laundry are free and there's a raucous bar attached. To find the hostel, walk up the east side of Yaxiu Market and just keep going. ⚅ Off Sanlitun Bei Lu • Map H2 • 6417 2597 • Subway: Dong Si Shi Tiao • ¥¥ • www.poachers.com.cn

10 Zhaolong International Youth Hostel

A quiet option despite the proximity to Sanlitun bar district. Dorms are decently tidy and guests have access to a self-catering dining room, games room, and bike rentals. The front door is locked at 1am nightly. ⚅ 2 Gongren Tiyuchang Bei Lu • Map H2 • 6597 2299 • Subway: Dong Si Shi Tiao • ¥¥ • www.greatdragon hotel.com.cn

Phrase Book

The Chinese language belongs to the Sino-Tibetan family of languages and uses characters which are ideographic – a symbol is used to represent an idea or an object. Mandarin Chinese, known as Putonghua in mainland China, is fairly straightforward as each character is monosyllabic. Traditionally, Chinese is written in vertical columns from top right to bottom left, however the Western style is widely used. There are several romanization systems; the Pinyin system used here is the official system in mainland China. This phrase book gives the English word or phrase, followed by the Chinese script, then the Pinyin for pronunciation.

Guidelines for Pronunciation

Pronounce vowels as in these English words:

a	as in "father"
e	as in "lurch"
i	as in "see"
o	as in "solid"
u	as in "pooh"
ü	as the French u or German ü (place your lips to say oo and try to say ee)

Most of the consonants are pronounced as in English. As a rough guide, pronounce the following consonants as in these English words:

c	as ts in "hats"
q	as ch in "cheat"
x	as sh in "sheet"
z	as ds in "heads"
zh	as j in "Joe"

Mandarin Chinese is a tonal language with four tones, represented in Pinyin by one of the following marks ˉ ´ ˇ ` above each vowel – the symbol shows whether the tone is flat, rising, falling and rising, or falling. The Chinese characters do not convey this information: tones are learnt when the character is learnt. Teaching tones is beyond the scope of this small phrase book, but a language course book with a cassette or CD will help those who wish to take the language further.

Dialects

There are many Chinese dialects in use. It is hard to guess exactly how many, but they can be roughly classified into one of seven large groups (Mandarin, Cantonese, Hakka, Hui etc.), each group containing a large number of more minor dialects. Although all these dialects are quite different – Cantonese uses six tones instead of four – Mandarin or Putonghua, which is mainly based on the Beijing dialect, is the official language. Despite these differences all Chinese people are more or less able to use the same formal written language so they can understand each other's writing, if not each other's speech.

In an Emergency

Help!	请帮忙！	Qing bangmang
Stop!	停住！	Ting zhu
Call a doctor!	叫医生！	Jiao yisheng
Call an ambulance!	叫救护车！	Jiao jiuhuche
Call the police!	叫警察！	Jiao jiingcha
Fire!	火！	Huo
Where is the hospital/police station?	医院/警察分局在哪里？	Yiyuan/jingcha fenju zai nali？

Communication Essentials

Hello	你好	Nihao
Goodbye	再见	Zaijian
Yes/no	是／不是	shi/bushi
… not …	不是	bushi
I'm from…	我是 … 人	Wo shi … ren
I understand	我明白	Wo mingbai
I don't know	我不知道	Wo bu zhidc
Thank you	谢谢你	Xiexie ni
Thank you very much	多谢	Duo xie
Thanks (casual)	谢谢	Xiexie
You're welcome	不用谢	Bu yong xie
No, thank you	不，谢谢你	Bu, xiexie ni
Please (offering)	请	Qing
Please (asking)	请问	Qing wen
I don't understand	我不明白	Wo Bu ming
Sorry/Excuse me!	抱歉／对不起	Booqian/duibuqi
Could you help me please? (not emergency)	你能帮助我吗？	Ni neng bar zhu wo me

Useful Phrases

My name is ….	我叫 …	Wo jiao …
Goodbye	再见	Zaijian
What is (this)?	(这）是什么？	(zhe) shi shenme?
Could I possibly have …? (very polite)	能不能请你给我 …?	Neng bunei qing ni ge wo …
Is there … here?	这儿有 … 吗？	Zhe'r you …
Where can I get …?	我在哪里可以得到 …?	Wo zai na la de dao …?
How much is it?	它要多少钱？	Ta yao duo qian?
What time is …?	… 什么时间？	… shenme shijian
Cheers! (toast)	干杯	Ganbei
Where is the restroom/toilet?	卫生间／洗手间在哪里？	Weishengjian/Xishoujian zh nali?

Signs

open	开	kai
closed	关	guan
entrance	入口	rukou
exit	出口	chukou
danger	危险	weixian
emergency exit	安全门	anquanme
information	信息	xinxi
restroom/toilet	卫生间	Weishengjian
(men)	洗手间	Xishoujian
(women)	（男士）（女士）	(nanshi) (nüshi)
men	男士	nanshi
women	女士	nüshi

...ney

	银行	yinhang
...t card	信用卡	xinyongka
...ency exchange	外汇兑换处	waihui
		duihuanchu
...rs	美元	meiyuan
...nds	英镑	yingbang
	元	yuan

...ping in Touch

...re is a	电话在哪里?	Dianhua
...phone?		zai nali?
...I use your	我可以用你的	Wo keyi
...e?	电话吗?	yong nide
		dianhua ma?
...ile phone	手机	shouji
...card	卡	sim ka
..., this is ...	你好, 我是 ...	Nihao, wo shi
	航空	hangkong
...ail	电子邮件	dianzi youjian
	传真	chuanzhen
...net	互联网	hulianwang
...card	明信片	mingxinpian
...office	邮局	youju
	邮票	youpiao
...phone card	电话卡	dianhua ka

...pping

...re can I	我可以在哪里	Wo keyi
...y ...?	买到 ...?	zai nali
		maidao ...?
...es this cost?	这要多少钱?	Zhe yao duo-
		shao qian?
...much!	太贵了!	Tai gui le!
...ou have?	你有 ... 吗?	Ni you ... ma?
...I try this	我可以试穿吗?	Wo keyi shi
		chuan ma?
...se show	请给我看看那	Qing gei wo
...that.	个。	kankan na ge.

...htseeing

...re is ...?	... 在哪里?	... zai nali?
...do I	我怎么到 ...?	Wo zenme
...to ...?		dao ...?
...ar?	远不远?	Yuan bu
		yuan?
	桥	qiao
...enter	城市	chengshi
	市中心	shi zhongxin
...ens	花园	huayuan
...ntain	山	shan
...um	博物馆	bowuguan
...e	宫殿	gongdian
	公园	gongyuan
	港口	gangkou
	江, 河	jiang, he
	废墟	feixu
...ping area	购物区	gouwu qu
...e	神殿	shendian
...e	街	jie
	寺庙	si/miao
...e	镇	zhen
	村	cun
...e	动物园	dongwuyuan
	北	bei

south	南	nan
east	东	dong
west	西	xi
left/right	左 / 右	zuo/you
straight ahead	一直向前	yizhi
		xiangqian

Getting Around

airport	机场	jichang
bicycle	自行车	zixingche
I want to rent	我想租一辆自	Wo xiang
a bicycle	行车。	zu yiliang
		zixingche.
ordinary bus	公共汽车	gonggong
		qiche
express bus	特快公共汽车	tekuai gong-
		gong qiche
minibus	面包车	mianbaoche
main bus	公共汽车总站	gonggong qiche
station		zong zhan
Which bus	哪一路公共汽	Nayilu gong-
goes to ...?	车到 ... 去?	gong qiche
		dao ... qu?
Please tell me	请告诉我在哪	Qing gaosu
where to	里下车?	wo zai nali
get off?		xia che.
car	小汽车	xiaoqiche
ferry	渡船	duchuan
baggage room	行李室	xingli shi
one-way ticket	单程票	dancheng piao
return ticket	往返票	wangfan piao
taxi	出租车	chuzuche
ticket	票	piao
ticket office	售票处	shoupiao chu
timetable	时刻表	shikebiao

Accommodations

air-conditioning	空调	kongtiao
bath	洗澡	xizao
check-out	退房	tui fang
deposit	定金	dingjin
double bed	双人床	shuangren
		chuang
hair drier	吹风机	chuifeng ji
room	房间	fangjian
economy room	经济房	jingji fang
key	钥匙	yaoshi
front desk	前台	qiantai
single/twin	单人 /	danren/
room	双人房	shuangren fang
single beds	单人床	danren chuang
shower	淋浴	linyu
standard room	标准房间	biaozhun
		fangjian
deluxe suite	豪华套房	haohua
		taofang

Eating Out

May I see the	请给我看看菜	Qing gei wo
menu?	单。	kankan
		caidan
Is there a set	有没有套餐?	You meiyou
menu?		taocan?
I'd like	我想要 ...	Wo xiang yao
May I have	请给我这个。	Qing gei wo
one of those?		zhege
I am a	我是素食者。	Wo shi
vegetarian		sushizhe

Waiter/waitress!	服务员！	Fuwuyuan!
May I have a fork/knife/ spoon	请给我一叉 / 刀 / 汤匙。	Qing gei wo yiba cha/ dao/tangshi
May we have the check please.	请把帐单开给我们。	Qing ba zhangdan kaigei women
breakfast	早餐	zaocan
buffet	自助餐	zizhucan
chopsticks	筷子	kuaizi
dinner	晚餐	wancan
to drink	喝	he
to eat	吃	chi
food	食品	shipin
full (stomach)	饱	bao
hot/cold	热 / 冷	re/leng
hungry	饿	e
lunch	午餐	wucan
set menu	套餐	taocan
spicy	酸辣	suan la
hot (spicy)	辣	la
sweet	甜	tian
mild	淡	dan
Western food	西餐	xi can
restaurant	餐馆	canguan
restaurant (upscale)	饭店	fandian

Food

apple	苹果	pingguo
bacon	咸肉	xianrou
bamboo shoots	笋	sun
beancurd	豆腐	doufu
bean sprouts	豆芽	dou ya
beans	豆	dou
beef	牛肉	niurou
beer	啤酒	pijiu
bread	面包	mianbao
butter	黄油	huangyou
chicken	鸡	ji
crab	蟹	xie
duck	鸭	ya
eel	鳗	man
egg	蛋	dan
eggplant	茄子	qiezi
fermented soybean paste	酱	jiang
fish	鱼	yu
fried egg	炒蛋	chao dan
fried tofu	油豆腐	you doufu
fruit	水果	shuiguo
fruit juice	果汁	guo zhi
ginger	姜	jiang
ice cream	冰淇淋	bingqilin
meat	肉	rou
melon	瓜	gua
noodles	面	mian
egg noodles	鸡蛋面	jidan mian
wheat flour noodles	面粉面	mianfen mian
rice flour noodles	米粉面	mifen mian
omelet	煎蛋饼	jiandanbing
onion	洋葱	yangcong
peach	桃子	taozi
pepper	胡椒粉，辣椒	hujiaofen, lajiao
pickles	泡菜	paocai

pork	猪肉	zhurou
potato	土豆	tudou
rice	米饭	mifan
rice crackers	爆米花饼干	baomihua bing
rice wine	米酒	mi jiu
salad	色拉	sela
salmon	鲑鱼，大马哈鱼	guiyu, dama
salt	盐	yan
scallion	韭葱	jiucong
seaweed	海带	haidai
shrimp	虾	xia
soup	汤	tang
soy sauce	酱油	jiangyou
squid	鱿鱼	youyu
steak	牛排	niupai
sugar	糖	tang
vegetables	蔬菜	shucai
yoghurt	酸奶	suannai

Drinks

beer	啤酒	pijiu
black tea	红茶	hong cha
coffee (hot)	（热）咖啡	(re) kafei
green tea	绿茶	lü cha
iced coffee	冰咖啡	bing kafei
milk	牛奶	niunai
mineral water	矿泉水	kuang quan
orange juice	橙汁	cheng zhi
wine	葡萄酒	putaojiu

Numbers

0	零	ling
1	一	yi
2	二	er
3	三	san
4	四	si
5	五	wu
6	六	liu
7	七	qi
8	八	ba
9	九	jiu
10	十	shi
11	十一	shiyi
12	十二	shier
20	二十	ershi
21	二十一	ershi yi
22	二十二	ershi er
30	三十	sanshi
40	四十	sishi
100	一百	yi bai
101	一百零一	yi bai ling yi
200	二百	er bai

Time

Monday	星期一	xingqiyi
Tuesday	星期二	xingqi'er
Wednesday	星期三	xingqisan
Thursday	星期四	xingqisi
Friday	星期五	xingqiwu
Saturday	星期六	xingqiliu
Sunday	星期天	xingqitian
today	今天	jintian
yesterday	昨天	zuotian
tomorrow	明天	mingtian

General Index

Acknowledgments

The Author

Andrew Humphreys is a travel writer and editor who recently spent six months exploring Beijing.

Produced by
BRAZIL STREET
Editorial Nancy Pellegrini, Andrew Humphreys
Design Gadi Farfour
Main Photographer Chen Chao
Photography co-ordinator and Factchecking Amanda Mengpo Li
Proofreader Ferdie McDonald

AT DORLING KINDERSLEY
Series Publisher Douglas Amrine
Publisher Managers Vivien Antwi, Jane Ewart
Senior Editor Hugh Thompson
Cartography co-ordinator Casper Morris
Picture Research Rachel Barber, Ellen Root
DTP Designer Natasha Lu
Production Linda Dare

Additional Photography

Demetrio Carrasco, Eddie Gerald, Ian O'Leary, Colin Sinclair, Linda Whitwam

Picture Credits

Dorling Kindersley would like to thank all the many establishments covered in this book for their assistance and kind permission for the porducers to take photographs.
Placement Key: t–top; tl–top left; tr–top right; tc–top center; tcl–top center left; c–center; cr–center righ b–bottom; bl–bottom left; bottom right.

ALAMY IMAGES: Pat Behnke 38tr David Crausby 107tl; PANORAMA STOCK / Li Jiangshu 98tl; Matthew Wellings 34tr;
CENTRO: 62tr;
CHINA ART SEASONS: 24–5c;
CORBIS: Bettmann 33r; Burstein Collection 32tl; Hulton-Deutsch Collection 32tc; Kelly-Mooney Photography 12bc; Liu Liqun 99t; Reuters 35bl;
GETTY IMAGES: Hulton 32c; The Image Bank/Andrea Pistolesi 8 -9; Photographer's Choice/John Warde 28br; Taxi / Walter Bibikow 4–5;
GREEN T. HOUSE: 60tl;
HATSUNE: 89tl;
IMAGINECHINA: Wu Changquing 2 27; Long Hai 38br;
KEMPINSKI HOTELS: 29t, 114, 112
OFFICE FOR METROPOLITAN ARCHITECTURE: 40tl, 40tr, 40br;
PHOTOS12.COM: Panoramic Stock 28–9;
RED GATE GALLERY: 84tr.

All other images are © Dorling Kindersle For more information see *www.dkimage com*.